The Motorcycle Club

John Edward Bunch II

Black Dragon

National President

Mighty Black Sabbath Motorcy

Club Nation

A Breed Apart

Since 1974 and Still Strong...........///

www.blacksabbathmc.com

www.blacksabbathmagazine.com

404.692.0336

blackdragon@blacksabbathmc.com

Bunch Publishing

4575 Webb Bridge Road #5363

Alpharetta, Ga 30005

G000124235

s.

Love, Honor, Perseverance, Duty, Courage, Loyalty, Ethics

Edited by

- Christin Chapman
- Robert 'Bob' Coleman
- Robert 'Bob' Schultz
- Tanisha Knight (my darling daughter)

First Edition, Second Printing May 2016

The Motorcycle Club Public Relations Officer's Bible

By, John Edward Bunch II 'Black Dragon' BSFFBS

Motorcycle Club Public Relations Officer's Bible is the second book of the Motorcycle Club Bible series. It is a *how to* manual that teaches Motorcycle Club Public Relations Officers how to become Guardians of the motorcycle club's reputation and manager of its publics.

<u>Bunch Publishing</u>
Motorcycle Club Education Division

Copyright © 2016 by

John 'Black Dragon' Edward Bunch II
National President

The Motorcycle Club Public Relations Officer's Bible
Library of Congress Control Number: **2016904104**
International Standard Book Number: **978-0-692-66577-0**
◊◊◊

For information about special discounts for bulk purchases or club purchases please contact Bunch Publishing at 404.692.0336 or blackdragon@blacksabbathmc.com.

Black Dragon can speak at your live event. For more information or to book an event contact Bunch Publishing at 404.692.0336 or blackdragon@blacksababthmc.com.

www.PROsBible.com
MC PROs Bible on Facebook
◊◊◊

Dedication

Above all, I want to thank God.

To my editors, Bob Coleman, Bob Schultz, Christin Chapman, Daisy Phillips and my darling daughter Tanisha Bunch.

To my beloved mother and best friend who is now deceased Anese Yvonne Bunch 1942 - 1997 RIP

To my dearly loved and now deceased Pitt/Labrador whom I still cannot seem to let go from my heart, Hope Magda Charity Warrigal, Mighty Dogg of Dogs the Benevolent, Great Magnificent Conqueror the Lion Hearted, Bunch I, Conquering Dog of the Tribe of Judah, Elect of God! And yes, you lived up to every bit of that name. 2004 - 2013 RIP

To my love Noshera Pitts who owns my heart.

To Master Chief Tommy 'Hogman' Lewis for years of guidance.

To The Father of the Mighty Black Sabbath MC Nation Paul 'Pep' Perry.

To Kingfish and Beast of the Flaming Knights MC Nation, and to Foxy of the MC Professional Convention. Thanks for the speaking opportunity at the 2015 PROC

Special thanks to Terri (Sexy Ass Teacher) Benn and Monica 'Poochie' Pete.

Foreword

In many of today's modern MCs, after the President, the Motorcycle Club (MC) Public Relations Officer (PRO) represents the public face of the MC. Working under direction of the President and the executive board, the PRO is the de facto guardian of the MC's reputation and manager of its publics. Thus, it is responsible for disseminating communications of the MC to other MC Nations and communicating the public messages of the MC to the SET, governmental agencies, law enforcement, media, and civilian communities. To that end, today's PRO should reach for excellence in performing their duties to ensure a positive public image is achieved and maintained throughout the daily operations of the MC.

As the office PRO is new to the MC Set and not acknowledged by many historical or traditional MCs there is much ambiguity as to what the official duties of the PRO are. The *newness* of this position invites individuals responsible for carrying out the PRO's duties to speculate wildly about how to do the job leaving no clear definition upon which to refer. Where no history exists to define these duties, there naturally are wide variances from MC to MC as to how PROs should perform their jobs. The MC PRO's Bible attempts to set minimum standards of performance, education, and professional conduct that should be expected of the office of PRO. It uses the approach of discovering what Public Relations (PR) professionals do in corporate America and relates, assigns, and associates those duties to similar requirements of the MC.

As PRO you will guide your President and executive board in utilizing best practices and communication strategies when:

- Disseminating information about club events
- Establishing relationships with other MC Nations
- Communicating the MC's goal, mission and direction to interested parties
- Documenting the MC's charitable activities
- Creating a communication plan for crisis management
- Providing content for the MC's websites and social media portals
- Documenting the MC's history

The MC PRO's Bible was written as a guide to help you to prepare effective communication strategies for your MC. It will not answer all of your questions but it will help you to formulate a competent communication plan that will present a strong, successful, positive, and professional public image for your MC.

My Qualifications:

As the National President of the Mighty Black Sabbath Motorcycle Club Nation for the past seven years (at the writing of this book) I have spent 27 years on the MC Biker Set. I have also served as a National Enforcer, and President/Founder of the Atlanta chapter. As National President I've launched more than 15 chapters since 2009 and expanded the reach of the BSMC Nation from coast to coast. In accomplishing my responsibilities for the MC, I have had to operate extensively in the realm of PR to defend her reputation and manage her publics. As a Prospect my gift of writing helped the club early on. I edited and updated the bylaws at the request of The Father. In the late 1990's I led the MC's battle against the City of San Diego to keep her doors open when the city attorney decided to shut the clubhouse down. I have had to manage the MC's PR efforts through many difficult and challenging crisis throughout the years; from the murder of a local chapter President, club civil wars, and murders of patrons in and around our national chapters, to police harassment, community petitions, and outrageous international news reports. I have also had the pleasure of representing the MC through high times and excellent achievement.

Indeed, I was a PRO long before there was ever such an office in any MC, and as a National President, I lead our nation as a PRO (of sorts) every day. I have learned that once a PRO always a PRO. In my estimation a savvy PRO is destined to one day become President or National President. Professionally, it seems my life's experiences guided me to the point where I could write this book. I have owned and published more than 10 magazines, owned and designed 20+ blogs and websites, written articles for national magazines, plied my skills as an international model photographer, served as Editor in Chief of the San Diego Newslink Newspaper (published by William Patrick DeShields) and worked for over 15 years as a Senior Technical Writer for multi-national telecommunications companies. My Bachelors of Science Degree is from Southern Illinois University at Carbondale in Workforce Education, Training and Development. I have also traveled the world as a military and corporate senior technical trainer for over 25 years. Walk with me as I guide you to becoming an incredibly talented and organized communicator for your beloved MC Nation.

◊◊◊

"It is always a risk to speak to the press: they are likely to report what you say." – Hubert H. Humphrey

Who Should Read this Book?

It should be read by MC members and officers who are interested in the advancement of professional communications strategies for their Motorcycle Club Nations.

- MC Public Relations Officers
- MC Presidents
- MC Vice Presidents
- MC Secretaries
- MC Business Managers
- MC Sgt at Arms
- MC Web Masters
- MC Founders
- Full Patched Members

The PRO is the professional communicator of the MC. He/she is the guardian of the MC's reputation and the manager of its publics!

◊◊◊

When to Use this Book

Use this book as a reference manual to help you develop your communication strategies. In these chapters you will find templates, ideas, anecdotes and communications plans for various situations that MCs commonly face when dealing with their publics:

- Refer to various templates to write necessary correspondence
- Refer to tips to jog memory
- Refer to strategies to assemble communications plans

Where there is no competent leadership chaos will prevail...

JB11

Contents

CHAPTER ONE
PROs Rule

Welcome

Welcome to the world of professional public communications! If you have been elected PRO for your MC or are considering running for the office, this book is for you. Many people think being a PRO for an MC is a mundane job primarily concerned with discovering where all of the great Biker Set parties are then posting them on your MC's chat line for your members to see. However, the position of PRO is far more serious than that. This book will teach you how to become a superior PRO. The Motorcycle Club Public Relations Officer Bible will help you make the PRO real!

◊◊◊

Making the PRO Real

The position of PRO in today's modern MCs is possibly the most controversial position on the Biker Set. You simply will not find it in most traditional (old school) MCs or 1%er MC nations. In fact, the PRO may really only be prevalent on the Black Biker Set and may have wholly originated there. Strict traditionalists argue, on web sites and blogs across the country, that the PRO position is completely invalid and even dismiss MCs that have PROs as "B.S." "Popup" or "Sucka" MCs. One 2012 blog post that I once read (http://suckamcfree.blogspot.com/2012/03/mc-title-holders-good-bad-bullshit-and.html) stated "What the f*ck is a PRO but a glorified flyer dispenser." In an answer to another reply on his post the author also wrote, "No disrespect to any PRO's out there but a PRO is a myth. You're the Great Pumpkin. You're not real! Everyone in the club is a PRO. Get real or just git."

Others argue that the duties of the so called PRO are encompassed in the duties of the traditional Secretary's position. In fact, the *Motorcycle Club Riding Club Education* website/blog (*http://www.rcvsmc.net/id5.html*) states the position of the Secretary as:

"Responsible for making and keeping all club chapter records, membership List, chapter bylaws, rules of order, standing rules, records of all committee appointments, all written reports, copies of all correspondence between the club and any outside person or organization, and meeting minutes. He is responsible for calling roll at the meetings. The Secretary must notify active members of special or emergency meetings, and must notify all the members of any appointments or elections in their absence."

If you focus on the clause in that statement of duties that says "correspondence between the club and any outside person or organization," there would seem to be no room for the PRO. The Secretary, it would seem, appears to be in control of all public facing interactions. That being said, still an ever increasing number of MCs across the United States have PROs and there doesn't seem to be a stemming of the tide coming any time soon. More clubs continue to open up the PRO position and professional organizations are springing up to provide education and services for this group; that is working hard to gain recognition on the MC Biker Set. For example, take the MC Professional Convention that started as the PROC in Philadelphia, PA in 2004 (http://www.proconvention.com/). It began as a "Get-Together" for PROs from urban motorcycle clubs predominantly in the North Eastern portion of the country—to speak about current affairs within the MC Community and to fellowship. Today, the PROC that spawned from a small gathering of 100 or so bikers in a small bar in Philadelphia for a one-day event, has become a three-day weekend encompassing education, safety, maintenance clinics, guest speakers and club officer breakout sessions. In fact, in the past few years the hugely successful PROC has sold out completely with hundreds of participating MCs sending thousands of delegates to network, learn, and matriculate. Also, PRO education remains heavy on the list of the conferences' objectives. It is obvious that the PRO position is expanding in both influence and professionalism on the MC Set among 99%er MC Nations.

Though hotly contested, the PRO is not going away! A bunch of folks writing negative articles and spitting viscous words of hate are not going to make the PRO stop working. So, let us make this clear. If you are a PRO, you are not a living a myth. You are not the Great Pumpkin. You are real! Though everyone in the club should be a club ambassador and act like a PRO, there is only one PRO! You are the PRO; and no one else!

So let us embrace your duties, responsibilities, skills, and agenda. Let us define your movement and give you the tools to successfully accomplish your mission. To hell with those who hate on what you do, would undermine your efforts, and seek to call your hard work meaningless. Let them do what they do in their MCs. You do what you need to do to advance the best interests of your Mighty MC Nation. Reject the naysayers and empower your vision. Today and forever more we make the PRO real!

◊◊◊

Defining the Pro

The PRO is the elected or appointed professional communicator of the MC with honed and dedicated skills in:

- Public Relations
- Media Management
- Marketing
- News Reporting
- Crisis Management
- Networking
- Public Speaking and Interviewing
- Documentation
- Accurate Measurements of Historical Milestones

What is the PRO?
The PRO is the guardian of the MC's reputation and the manager of its

publics!

The PRO will work hand in hand with the President and the Executive Committee in:

- O Planning, developing, and implementing PR communication strategies
- O Liaising with members, the Executive Committee, and the President to develop communications strategies for various events
- O Liaising with and answering inquiries from media, individuals, MCs and other organizations; often via telephone, email, websites, and social media
- O Researching, writing, and distributing press releases to targeted media for MC activities, charity events, runs, and damage control
- O Collating and analyzing media coverage
- O Writing and editing in-house magazines, newsletters, President and officer speeches, articles, reports, and external facing documentation
- O Preparing and supervising the production of publicity brochures, handouts, direct mail leaflets, flyers promotional videos, photographs, films, and multimedia programs
- O Devising and coordinating photo opportunities
- O Organizing events including: press conferences, exhibitions, clubhouse open days, and press/media tours
- O Content management, updating and editing information on the MC's websites and BLOGs
- O Managing and updating information and engaging with users on the MC's social media sites such as Twitter, Instagram, and Facebook
- O Sourcing and managing speaking and sponsorship opportunities for the President and the MC
- O Fostering community relations through events such as picnics, charitable giving, parades, charity runs, open days, and through involvement in community initiatives

- Managing the PR aspect of a potential crisis situation in which the MC or members are involved
- Managing MC to MC communications, networking and relationships
- Notifying MC of all outside activities the MC may be interested in attending
- Spearheading the development of the yearly travel and events calendar
- Publicly representing the MC when tasked to do so by the President; where it is appropriate
- Managing the press when necessary to run interview questions asked by reporters of the President
- Comprising a comprehensive marketing program to present the Executive Committee for all club functions, dances, and fund raising activities

The PRO will have to work diligently to master the aforementioned duties. It will take a combination of self-study, training, and personal development to excel as a professional communicator for the MC. If handled correctly the MC will be well represented by the PRO Master Communicator.

CHAPTER TWO
The World of Public Relations

Managing Reputation

According to www.PRQuickStart.org the number one contribution public relations (PR) professionals make to their companies, in the corporate world, is reputation management. When you are the PRO of an MC you should operate likewise, protecting and expanding the MC's reputation with every decision you make.

But what exactly is reputation management? Have you ever known an MC that has a terrible reputation with law enforcement or its neighbors? Often you stay away from their clubhouse because *just going there* can get you a ticket. You can immediately pick up a bad reputation simply from hanging out at that MC. You see an MC's reputation can make or break it in a community. Your job is to manage the MC's reputation to keep it from going bad or to do everything you can to clean it up if it has gone bad.

Reputation management works to create positive feelings about an MC by highlighting excellent things the MC does such as membership commitment, philanthropy, public works; and to advise the MC to steer away from negative stereotypes- racing through the neighborhood, revving engines, creating a nuisance, and warring with visiting MCs at club events.

Reputation management has become more and more critical as the speed of communication has increased. MCs' reputations can be demolished in the wake of a breaking scandal or a violent clash between Full Patch members of the MC and a citizen at a stop light. Scandals can spread unbelievably fast between camera-phones, blogs, and the twenty-four hour news cycle. Presidents who find themselves in hot water can bring down an entire MC's reputation as well because the reputation of the MC is built upon the back of its President. Individual members who are on their own but commit bad acts while wearing the MC's colors, can also make things bad for the entire MC. There is no "I" in MC. Every Full Patch member associated with the MC can make or break its reputation in a nanosecond. Cyber-bullying on social media, for example, can go viral and bring an MC to its knees exposing it to negative national attention from news agencies and federal law enforcement. For these reasons, seasoned and/or astute PROs with experience, or a propensity towards reputation and crisis management, are becoming increasingly valuable to today's MCs.

The most important thing to remember about reputation management is that not enough can be said about developing a positive MC reputation through ethical MC practices, good word of mouth, happy members, and charitable contributions in the first place. These high standards from the gate can pay real dividends and should be the goal of any 99%er MC. More and more, those dividends are quantifiable. A sharp PRO will know how to capitalize on every positive event the MC sponsors, and bring the right eyeballs to these activities to build the MC's credibility. He/she will advise the MC at every level from the President and Executive Committee to Full Patch members, Prospects, and Hang-Arounds that the reputation of the MC should always be protected; and train them with a tool chest full of strategies.

PROs use all forms of media and communications to build, maintain, and manage the reputation of their MCs. These range from public bodies or services to businesses and voluntary organizations.

PROs communicate key messages to *defined* target audiences in order to establish and maintain goodwill and understanding between the MC and its publics.

PROs monitor publicity and conduct research to find out the concerns and expectations of its publics. PROs then report and explain the findings to the President and the Executive Committee.

Finally, PROs create a strategic plan to accomplish communication goals that are in the best interests of the MC.

The intensity of the PRO role will vary from MC to MC. It will surely be what you will make of the position. You can simply post information about MC parties, design flyers, and post events on your club's bulletin board; or you can become fully involved in the public direction of your MC providing sound advice and a clear public direction for your members.

◊◊◊

Working Hours

If you don't want to work long and hard hours do not choose to pursue the position of PRO. The working hours can be longer than most other officer positions, with the exception of the President and VP. The workload includes lots of research, networking, counseling, conversations, travel, writing, and compilation of information above and beyond the MC's monthly or weekly meetings. You will also attend runs, dances, annuals, and events of other MCs as well as your own MC. These events will occur in the evening and on weekends- late into the night.

During these events you might accompany the President and be responsible for introducing him to other MC Presidents/dignitaries and guiding him in his networking forays. You will rub elbows with the VIPs of the MC world to include national officers, founders, radio, television personalities, the media, other MC PROs, and traditional MC Secretaries.

You will create or edit flyers and other promotional materials to provide to members for distribution, and then monitor that distribution and its impact on the targeted market.

You will press the agenda of the MC by interacting with PROs from other MCs across the nation and perhaps internationally, with written correspondence, emails, text messages, calendar sharing, and a plethora of other informational communication standards. With the exception of the President and perhaps the VP, no one will pitch the MCs events, runs, celebrations, annuals, parties, and reputation harder than you. Prepare yourself for the hardest unpaid job of your life! It will cost you some time and will be a heavy responsibility if you do the job the right way.

◊◊◊

Qualifications for the PRO

No set qualifications are required to become a PRO for an MC except for the desire to learn and become competent at defending, advancing, and building the MC's reputation. There are some PR courses you can take online and books you can read that will help you gain an inside track to understanding the various complexities of the position. Though this book may be one of few resources that will specifically address PR for motorcycle clubs, general reading is still very helpful as it can apply to many MC situations.

◊◊◊

Skills Required for the PRO

Though there aren't many qualifications that you will need to have to get started there are some skills you should possess if you are going to be able to hit the ground running:

- Excellent communication, interpersonal, and writing skills
- Drive, competence, flexibility, and willingness to learn
- Excellent organizational and time management skills with the ability to multitask
- Ability to cope with stress and excel under high pressure environments
- Creativity, imagination, and initiative
- Teamwork and team-building skills
- Analytical and problem-solving skills
- Solid understanding of MC protocol, club bylaws, and Biker Set traditions
- Solid understanding of Biker Set current affairs

◊◊◊

What to Expect

A good working PRO becomes involved in the entirety of the MC advising members and officers, at every turn. You must earn the MC's trust by proving that you are the professional communicator who best knows how to get its message before the public in a manner that is in the best interests of the MC. For instance:

Case Scenario 1:

The MC decides to buy a clubhouse in a new neighborhood.

Response: You begin dropping press releases in local newspapers that highlight positive contributions of the MC to its last community, several months before the move. You could also have flyers distributed in the neighborhood inviting the community the new clubhouse for an 'open day'. At the clubhouse you may have pamphlets there that visitors could pick up that explained the 42 year old history of the MC and highlights the military service and veteran status of ninety-five percent of the Full Patch members of the MC.

Case Scenario 2:

The police near your clubhouse have taken a negative stand against the MC. In response to neighbor complaints about noise, racing through the streets, and engine revving; they are pulling everything over that enters or leaves your clubhouse. Now bikers are beginning to spread rumors that your MC is not the place to be because there is a good likelihood that a visitor could easily go to jail in your area.

Response: Knowing immediate action is necessary to protect the MC's interests you consult with the President and the Executive Committee, and recommend a plan to fine and suspend members who burnout in front of the MC and hot dog in the neighborhood. Then, you write a plan and a speech for the President to use to go to all of the MC's in the area explaining to them the need for restraint and good road practices while visiting your clubhouse because of the ongoing police enforcement actions. The speech also advises clubs that if their members hot dog while leaving your club house they will be banned and asked not to return. Finally, you arrange a meeting between the police chief and your President to discuss the steps the MC has taken to get law enforcement sanctions lifted from the clubhouse.

Case Scenario 3:

Your MC regularly feeds the homeless and builds homes for Habitat for Humanity.

Response: You write press releases and media releases to build the brand and credibility of your MC.

Case Scenario 4:

Your President is invited to speak at the PRO Convention in January.

Response: You begin helping him write and prepare his speech, Power Point presentation, and handouts.

Case Scenario 5:

You write and prepare stories for your MC's online magazine and conduct interviews of members who have noteworthy accomplishments (I.E., www.blacksabbathmagazine.com).

Response: You recognize all membership achievements that are positive on *every* level. For example, "Black Sabbath Nation would like to honor our brother Gopher who was awarded the Nomad patch..." And, "Black Sabbath Nation recognizes and congratulates the following prospects for crossing over to the Full Patch brotherhood..."

Emphasize major *and* minor. There are no small achievements. You list prospect detail as well as Full Patch member decorations. You do not want to miss a thing, thus, causing incentive for members to look to your magazine or publications for the 'what's happening'. If your club has done charity work, habitat for humanity-type work; if your club members helped an old lady cross the street-document it in the e-zine.

As an insider in the MC world you should offer virtually real-time breaking news on the motorcycle set. With this insider upper hand, you are able to generate your own media source. Make it your business for bikers to check your magazine daily just like our parents did the evening news growing up.

Include breaking news on sets that are not your own. On general principal, it is fair to say that rather the website you nurture is exclusive to your MC or not, reporting biker news outside of your set is imperative to your own club. If there is warfare in the neighboring MCs all of your members would be eager to know as they too are affected by such. You will be the one to bring it to them; one stop shop.

Case Scenario 6:

An incident at your clubhouse sparks a terse interview from an international news agency of your President.

Response: You work with your President to get his talking points in order and the mission statement of the MC memorized. You throw tough questions at him in practice sessions to get him ready for the press interview.

Case Scenario 7:

A crisis between your MC and another results in a series of investigative news reports.

Response: You write competing counter-stories and updates on your MC's website.

Case Scenario 8:

Your MC is preparing for its yearly annual dance.

Response: You design the flyers, post the event on websites, put together a list of Presidents for your President to call for support/attendance, call other MC PROs within you network to seek their aid, advise the MC as to which advertisement to purchase, contact celebrity entertainer's management to setup negotiations for acquiring their services, assemble the guest sign in books, and release media kits to the press.

Case Scenario 9:

Your VP writes a letter of condolence to another MC after the passing of their founder.

Response: You edit the letter and give it back to the VP for revising. After you and the VP have gotten the letter prepared you approve it for release to the public.

Case Scenario 10:
You write a Wikipedia article of the history of your MC to record, for posterity, the noble and mighty contributions your MC has made to the greater MC community.

Response: You learn the complex specifications and language code required to write a Wikipedia approved article. Learn requirements to successfully submit an article to the review board. Finally, see your article through to the publishing stage.

CHAPTER THREE
PUBLIC RELATIONS 101

Thinking Public Relations

The conundrum of PR is that to master it, you must master its tentacles that extend in all directions. Though, at first, that task may seem unwieldy; a thoughtful and deliberate process paired with organization will always see you through. So, do not become overwhelmed as you begin to embark upon this part of your MC career. Make tasks lists and mark things off one at a time. For any function you may have to perform there may be several disciplines you will have to employ- each requiring a different skill from one of the PR tentacles; hence the importance of mastering them all. For instance, for an event you may have to:

- Establish communications to media outlets
- Design press passes and assign the press to a 'media only' area
- Coordinate MC to MC networking for the President
- Setup photography and interview sessions
- Write and distribute press releases and media kits
- Coordinate with police security officials for the event
- Ensure guest speakers and VIPs are tended to with guest

rooms, room service, guides, and schedules
- Marketing for the event including flyer design, distribution, and venue planning

As you can see this list can go on and on. The most important thing is to begin thinking public relations and how you want to drive public opinion while tackling your lists and accomplishing your duties.

◊◊◊

Public Relations Is Not Advertising

According to the Public Relations Society of America (PRSA); "Public relations helps an organization and its publics adapt mutually to each other."

PR is often confused with advertising. Like advertising, it seeks to inform, educate, and persuade to action. However, unlike advertising, which controls its message and media through paid placement; PR builds relationships and creates an ongoing dialogue, interaction, and involvement with an MC's target audiences and those who influence those audiences.

Because PR is not advertising, successful PR management does not cost a lot of money. You can manage and build the MC's reputation and its publics without a lot of spending; still accomplishing the same Biker Set participation in club runs and events as larger MCs that have hundreds of members and limitless cash flows.

PR Benefits vs. Advertising

	Control	Credibility	Cost
Advertising	High	Low	High
PR	Low	High	Low

<source>cfa.org/Portals/0/documents/iams_cat_pr_101.pdf

◊◊◊

Public Relations Is Strategic Communications

PR is a strategic communications process that helps manage, protect, and enhance the reputation of an MC and its members. It is:

- Simple
    - For instance, one call can earn media coverage for your event, charity ride, or to feed the homeless in a park.
- Cost-effective
    - The media coverage generated from that one call can reach thousands or even millions which is advertising that could never be paid for.
- Powerful
    - The right story with the right message can have an enormous impact building the reputation and credibility of your MC as pillars in the community-instead of the alternative.

◊◊◊

Public Relations Can Do Many Things

PR can:
- Build an image
- Reinforce and further an MC's reputation
- Raise awareness of an MC's good deeds
- Educate audiences about the MC culture
- Increase understanding
- Change behavior
- Build credibility
- Influence opinion-leaders
- Motivate an MC's public to action
- Build credibility

- Supports MC strategy
- Help create and enforce the MC's niche
- Track and manage special issues
- Extend the reach, frequency, and the message of an advertising campaign
- Help create a supportive environment

◊◊◊

Public Relations *Can't* Do Some Things

Although PR can accomplish a lot of things, there are some things PR cannot accomplish. PR cannot:

- Eliminate competition from other MCs
- Eliminate other's opinions
- Cover up bad news (although crisis management may mitigate bad news)
- Manipulate public opinion (although we all try!)
- Control the media or the message through paid placements
- Replace advertising or other marketing communications techniques
- Compensate for bad decisions, corrupt practices, poor or illegal MC behavior by members and officers

CHAPTER FOUR
PR Tools

Tools of the PR Trade

To be a good craftsman you must become skilled with the tools of your trade. The PRO's tools are vast and can be well deployed once mastered:

- Press releases, media alerts, and press conferences
  - ○ For timely/breaking news
- 'Backgrounders'
  - ○ Information letters to build relationships/educate
  - ○ Meetings designed to build relationships/educate
- Special events
  - ○ Planned meetings and shows
  - ○ Created events for key audiences
- By-lined articles
  - ○ Gives your MC's point of view on an issue
- Talking points
  - ○ Used to keep speakers and members on point during speeches and interviews

- Speeches
  - ○ Gives your MC's point of view on an issue
- "Pitch letters or calls to media
  - ○ Propose coverage
- Photos, B-roll videotape, and other visuals
  - ○ Materials given to media to help tell your story
- Brochures, newsletters, and other collateral
- Web site content
  - ○ Blogs, discussion boards, etc...

Possessing PR tools is great, but you should put some practice to using them. The following sections in this chapter will contain templates and exercises to help you prepare yourself to use your new found PR tools.

◊◊◊

The Press Releases

The press release is an important tool that you can use to drive positive messages about your MC to the public without having to spend money to do so. You can use a press release to get out in front of a bad story or to display the MC's good work before local or national media that the MC could never have afforded to get to by purchasing advertising. Press releases are also important because stories can be generated from them and appear in newspapers, magazines, and on television news stations. These stories can be used later to document the history of the MC when necessary (more about this later). You can also distribute press releases on social media and generate exploding traffic. Unlike a simple social media post, a press release will appear with formatted information that can drive interest and set it apart from what other MCs are doing potentially bringing it positive news coverage.

Another neat thing about a press release, is that even though a news agency might not show up to cover your event after you send them one, if your press release is good, they may write your story from the press release as though they were there and had covered the entire event! Your event's story and pictures would appear in their publication even though you never once saw a reporter. That is because some editors, publishers, and reporters (especially of small papers and publications, like the kinds you may be targeting) are lazy or overwhelmed. Many comb through press releases to publish stories as 'fillers' when they have space left in their publications they need to fill. That is a good time to have a well written press release just sitting there with a big fat juicy story "Local Biker Club Feeds the Homeless." Ha. Every MC needs at least one person who should know how to write a good press release and since you are the PRO, you are up.

There are some essential elements for your press releases:

1. **Press releases are always written like a news story; the way you want the story written after the event has happened**, even though they talk about an event that has not happened yet. Therefore, a reporter can use the press release in a story that happened last weekend in Monday's paper, even though he never showed up for the event. If you include a picture of the event it is all the better!

2. **Your story must be newsworthy.** Think of presenting your story in a way that is different than most. Think of something that will cause interest. What is different about why your poker run or why you are feeding the homeless? Maybe, yours is a poker run for homeless veterans suffering from PTSD. Keep in mind that a newsworthy release, in your mind, does not guarantee that it will be covered immediately, or at all, in your target publications. There are different levels of news that can be assigned to press releases. A Level I release is newsworthy, and it will have what the industry calls "customer references" and "industry analyst references". If the press release was about an MC that helped out a group home with a car wash, the group home could be considered the MC's customer as

it is benefiting from the MC's service. The story is talking about something more than just the MC- it is talking about the MC's customer. An industry analyst reference could be the mayor consequently saying how thankful the city is for the MC's help supporting the group home in the story.

For instance, in 2011 the BSMC gave bikes to the Atlanta fire department group home for disadvantaged children. The Fire Chief presented the MC with a freedom medal. This press release contained a customer reference (group home helped by the MC) and an industry analyst reference (the Fire Chief who analyzed the service and thanked the MC)].

Level I releases can be posted on a wire service and are typically covered by a publication somewhere.

A Level II release is also newsworthy but has only one type of reference such as a vendor, a customer, or an industry analyst. These releases are typically posted on a wire service and have over a fifty percent chance of being covered.

A Level III release is newsworthy and is basically an FYI to keep people up to date on your MC. An example might be winning a contest or giving away a motorcycle. The level III press release only talks about the MC and it lacks any other kind of reference. Level III press releases may be posted to the wire, but this type of release is typically mailed to your target editorial list. Level III releases have less than a fifty percent chance of being covered as they are looked at like pure advertisements by some, but they are important way to maintain editorial mind-share so send them anyway.

Wire services exist to provide stories that news organizations can pull down and add to their papers, publications, and news station feeds. A story you submit to a wire in New Mexico can be shared on a wire in Shanghai, China! If you are good about writing press releases and stories you should subscribe to news wires so you can submit your stories for coverage all over the world!

3. **Define Your Target Press List.** Your target press list consists of the names, addresses, phone, fax, and email addresses of

the key press and publications you'd like to cover your MC's event. Press lists can typically be divided into two parts which include: Tier 1 press, or press and freelance reporters who write for publications that publish weekly/bi-weekly; and Tier 2 press, or press that target monthly publications. Your Tier 1 and 2 press lists may include a variety of publication types. Trade press are reporters or editors of publications in your specific area of interest. For example, motorcycle magazines, online motorcycle magazines, and motorcycle blogs would be one of your target "trade" publication areas of interest. However, local newspapers that might not have a specific motorcycle area, but are hot on current events, are not necessarily in your trade list but are definitely where you may want to target an audience.

4. **When developing your target press list, make sure you determine who at the publication covers MC news.** Do not use a blanket distribution strategy to disseminate your press release to publications. It drives reporters and editors crazy. Develop your list by scouring publications in your area that cover events and news that is relevant to your MC and causes.

5. **The press release must be timely.** I've read that the most productive time to send out a press release is on a Tuesday or Wednesday before ten-o-clock a.m. This logically seems like these would be better times than busy Mondays or Friday afternoons, and perhaps better than on weekends.

6. **It must have quotes.** Your press release must include at least one quote and if at all possible that quote should come from a VIP like the President of the MC. A quote from the President signifies that the MC is invested in the article and stands behind its message. Preferably your release will have a couple of quotes for the journalist to pick and choose. Quotes are important because they are readable, they help convey the information in a press release in a less

formal manner and they add a human element to a story that might be very data or information heavy.

7. **It must inform**, rather than sell! The end goal of a press release is media coverage, which will lead to awareness of your MC's message, thus, could very likely to lead to a boost in paid customers showing up to your party. However, since the press release is meant for a journalist's eyes first, you cannot sound as if you're selling tickets to your dance right off the bat. Journalist's like information. They like facts and statistics. Journalists do not like biased promotional material, and they usually won't help you sell your product.

8. **It must have a vibrant or eye-catching headline.** Your headline determines whether or not your press release even gets acknowledged. Journalists receive scores of press releases every day. They cannot possibly read all of them in their entirety, so the headline is how you get your foot in the door. A good headline is succinct and tells the reader the essence of your story. *"MC X Rides for Charity Next Weekend"]* is not a good headline. *"MC X Rides for the Justice of Domestic Violence Moms Who's Children are taken from them!"* is better because it is specific, quantifiable, and tells the reader exactly what the press release is about.

9. **Include contact information for the press to receive additional information.** It is important that the press knows with whom to follow up with. So include MC contact information and a telephone number as well as an email address at the top of the press release under the heading. Contacts are typically going to be the President, maybe VP or other officer, and you; the PRO. Also make sure to have your MC's website listed (URL address).

There is a particular way that press releases must be sent to news agencies. Think of it as a language that, if not spoken, will leave your press release on a desk instead of being picked up and read. The AP Style Press Release template should always be used.

PRESS RELEASE TEMPLATE
AP STYLE
Letterhead
Company Logo

NEWS RELEASE (in bold)
February 19, 2013

FOR IMMEDIATE RELEASE

CONTACT INFO
NAME & TITLE
PHONE NO.
EMAIL

Title/Headline
Subhead
- space -

CITY, STATE (in all caps) - First paragraph text. Answer or address the "5 Ws" (who, what, where, when, why it's important). blah blah blah blah blah blah blah blah blah blah blah blah. More details. Supplemental information. blah blah blah blah blah blah blah blah blah blah blah blah maybe a quotation. Blah blah blah blah blah blah blah blah blah blah blah.

Boilerplate, aka company bio, mission, and contact info as the last thing.

- ######## -   (use pound signs to signal the end of the press release)
- more -   (use this if the release continues onto 2nd page)

Now after your press release is written you will need to send it off to your press list via fax or email. A level I or II press release can be submitted to http://www.prnewswire.com/ as well. Journalists log onto the newswires daily looking for areas of interest. Also, note that you can control the geographic areas and publications/media that receive your press release through the wire service's select distribution list. You can find links to wire services and other online PR organizations and services with relevant Internet searches.

Don not forget to add your press release to your Web site. Press release pages are typically added to the "Press Release" link, which is often a link under the "About Your MC" area of your home page. This is important because your press release invites people to your Web page, and because you don't want to miss any opportunities! Include hyperlinks in your press release that link to your site, and make sure your page is up-to-date and looking good!

Now let us examine closer, what a realistic press release would look like.

Black Sabbath MC Nation P.O. Box 9321 San Diego, CA 91211
619.333.3333
www.blacksabbathmc.com
PRO@blacksabbathmc.com

FOR IMMEDIATE RELEASE:

——.————————————-

Bikers Rescue Homeless Vets

Black Sabbath MC Repays Sacrifices While There's Still Time

San Diego, California —March 5, 2010 — The Mighty Black Sabbath Motorcycle Club Nation is in the business of rescuing homeless veterans off San Diego's mean streets. Friday, March 9th 2010 the 36 year old MC will begin its fifteenth season of its self-appointed mission, 'Operation No Vet Left Behind', at the 14th street sewer complex on the city's main sewer line (Carver Street) at 3:30 p.m. sharp. This important mission is embarked upon every Friday evening during the coldest months in San Diego. Full patch brothers of the MC ride into the darkest corners of the city's underside to bring food, clothing, medical supplies, bibles, and cash to homeless veterans that are languishing under bridges and in sewers in the forgotten sections of the city.

"If they need food we feed them hot meals from our feeding truck. If they need bedding we have brand new sleeping bags and cots for them. If they are broke we put $20 or $30 in their pockets. If they need medical we take them to the hospital, and if they want out, we take them to shelters and make sure they get counseling" said Black Sabbath MC Founder Paul 'Pep the Father' Perry.

"I might have starved to death, died from a drug overdose or worse, died—had it not been for the Black Sabbath brothers taking me off of the streets" said former homeless veteran Paul Revere. Paul is now recovered and owns a million dollar condo on Redondo Beach. He assists the Black Sabbath in their mission and is currently prospecting to become a member of the MC.

Two Goals to the Mission

The Black Sabbath MC has targeted two main goals in accomplishing its mission. The first is to alleviate the immediate suffering of homeless veterans by giving them food, medicine, bedding, money, and supplies to get them to a stable place both physically and mentally. This is called the "Stabilization Phase." The second goal after the "Stabilization Phase" is to provide life-changing services and life skills programs that empower disadvantaged veterans in the San Diego community to take their lives back and reclaim them from the bridges and sewers of the city. This is called the "No Vet Left Behind Phase."

"We are absolutely amazed and overwhelmed by the goodwill and philanthropic nature of the Mighty Black Sabbath MC Nation" said San Diego Mayor Will Rogers. "You normally hear such negative things about motorcycle clubs but the Black Sabbath MC continues to demonstrate to all why they are called 'A Breed Apart!' We absolutely could not have saved the lives of this many veterans over the past fifteen years without the MC," he said.

The Mighty Black Sabbath Motorcycle Club Nation was established in 1974 by seven black men who rode on Sundays. The original seven founding fathers used to meet in each other's garages every other Sunday until one day the wives revolted and shut down their garage access. Undaunted, the founding fathers acquired a clubhouse at 4280 Market street in San Diego, California and called themselves Black Sabbath MC, where they remained for 40 years. Today the Mighty Black Sabbath Motorcycle Club Nation accepts all races, religions, creeds and occupations. They are a non-violent MC with chapters nationwide devoted to riding motorcycles, big distances, rain, sleet or snow! They are also dedicated to giving back to the community through their dozens of charities nationwide. The 'Operation No Vet Left Behind' mission highlights the MC's efforts to make a positive impact on the lives of homeless veterans by changing and developing their minds, hearts, and spirits as it offers those in need a life altering bridge out of desperation and solitude.

"Most of us were Vets. We know how they feel. They sacrificed their lives for us. Now it's time for us to do the same for them" said San Diego MC Chapter President Old Iron Nutz.

"We think they are the best MC in the entire world and we hope they keep doing what they are doing for another fifteen years" said Mayor Will Rogers.

Social Networking
Launch www.blacksabbathmc.com and navigate to their 'Charitable Giving' tab to find links to their Facebook, Twitter, YouTube, Instagram, and Snap Chat sites to follow their national campaigns to give back from two wheels.

Media Contact:
Tom Ruffles PRO BSMC Nation San Diego Chapter
PROTRuffles@blacksabbathmc.com
619.333.3333

###

Your mission: You are to identify the elements of this press release based upon your study of the information above. Is this a level I or level II press release and why? Can you identify the customer reference, industry analyst reference and important quotes if they are there? If so, write a press release about something that is happening in your MC you that think is newsworthy and will build credibility for your MC. Test it out with someone in your MC for ways you can make it better. Then submit it to some papers and/or newswire and *see if YOU can get published*!!!

Case Study: In our history, several chapter club houses of the Mighty Black Sabbath MC Nation have come under heavy police pressure. One year, a certain chapter started getting harassed by a local police department. The police became so aggressive that they would walk up to the clubhouse and write parking tickets on the members' and visitors' motorcycles for "parking too close to the sidewalk". They hung outside of the clubhouse on club nights and pulled over every bike or car leaving the chapter to check for papers and documentation, to see if they were drunk, or to see if the officers could get enough evidence to make an arrest. The Black

Sabbath chapter quickly became the place not to be as the intimidation force was prevalent.

I began writing press releases and submitting to the local newspapers and the police chief every time the Black Sabbath conducted a charity run or other positive thing for the community. I also began submitting weekly press releases to the newspapers and to the police chief bitterly complaining about unfair policing practices. The city reversed itself under the pressure of the public press release and articles campaign. This stratagem has never failed us.

◊◊◊

The Media Alert

Media Alerts (AKA Press Alerts and Media Advisories) let the media know the facts about your event in a concise way. Media Alerts are a great way to get initial info to media, especially to the calendars of Listing Editors. If your event has a lot of elements to it, is extremely newsworthy, or has other elements such as interview opportunities; you can also write a Press Release. However, a media alert is **NOT** a press release. They are very different! So don't get them twisted.

The order of media alert information depends upon what you deem most important. For example:

- Who: List who at the top if your event has a notable name or guest of honor.
- What: List what at the top if the event itself is most important (8 times out of 10 this is the case).
- When: List when at the top if the date/time of the event is most important, such as a holiday party (this is unlikely; chances are this will still be in the what).
- Where: List where at the top if the location is most important (also unlikely).

- Why: List why at the top if the reason is the most important. This would be the case if, perhaps you are throwing a charity event.
- How: Is really uncommon and almost never used in media alerts, but if for some reason how you are throwing your event fits into the equation then it will be at the top.
- More Info: Additional info is always at the bottom of the media alert. (This is where you add a sentence or two that does not fit into any of the other categories. Additional info can be used for further instructions (dinner included in ticket price), where to buy tickets (tickets can be purchased at www.blacksabbathmc.com), or anything else pertinent to the event.

General Tips

- Don not include or attach anything. The media alert is quick and should not be weighed down.
- Keep it simple—choose a simple font in black.
- It is up to you where to include the price of the event. You can put it after additional info, but a good place to put it is after date and time. For example. When: Saturday, February 10, 2017 Doors open at 8:00 p.m. $20 Civilians $25 Patches.
- End media alerts with three italicized has tags (###) just like with press releases. This means there is no more information to follow on another page.
- Target media that will be interested in your event. Do some research on your contacts. Targeted media alerts sent to a few relevant journalists are more effective than a general blanket e-mail or fax bomb sent to a ton of journalists. Building relationships within the media is invaluable and can be key to the success of your events.
- The subject line should begin with the word "Media Alert", a colon, and something short about your event. Media is more likely to look at an email if they know it is meant for them and not spam. Example. Media Alert: Mighty Black Sabbath Motorcycle Club Nation San Diego Chapter 43rd

Annual Dance on February 10, 2017.

Media Alert Sample Composition:

Mighty Black Sabbath Motorcycle Club Nation
Tony Swarthy Public Relations Officer
PROTony@blacksabbathmc.com
619.333.3333

FOR IMMEDIATE RELEASE

MEDIA ALERT

Who:
Guest Entertainment Dongie Fresh and the Get Fresh Crew, The Time Pieces, MC Kid Capri Pants and Janet Jacksonville

What:
The Mighty Black Sabbath MC Nation San Diego Chapter 43rd Annual Dance Birthday Celebration! The weekend-long event features musical performances, vendor spaces, guest speakers, as well as junk food, liquor and dancing all night long!

When:
Meet and Greet Friday February 10, 2017 8: p.m. until, Annual Dance Saturday February 11, 2017 8: p.m. until, Free Breakfast Sunday morning February 12, 2017 8: a.m. until 12:00 p.m.

Where:
Qualcomb Stadium, 154 street San Diego Place Road. San Diego, CA 91201

Additional Info:
Tickets are available at www.blacksabbathmc.com
800.123.1234

For promotional photos, press passes and interviews, contact Tony Swarthy PRO at PROTony@blacksabbathmc.com
###

Can you identify the elements of this media alert? Can you distinguish the differences between a media alert and a press release? Do you know the reasons when one is used over the other? Can both be sent for the same event? Yes! Can you determine why "Who" was used first before "What" in the case of this sample media alert? Remember a press release is written as a story where as a media alert is written to call attention to an event.

Your mission: Write a media alert about an event that is happening within your MC. Get another PRO or perhaps the Secretary in your MC to evaluate it and make recommendations on how you can make it better!

◊◊◊

The Press Conference

Most times, the farther an MC can stay away from the press the better. News agencies and Hollywood have made lots of money, over the years depicting MCs as roving hordes of idiots storming through towns, raping women, selling drugs, gun running and pimping prostitutes. But the savvy PRO understands that managing the MC's publics sometimes involves artful interaction with a mostly biased press to achieve positive outcomes for the MC. When dealing with the press the PRO must give them positive snapshots of the MC that cannot be disputed or misinterpreted. These positive snapshots can result in positive stories that uplift the reputation of the MC instead of harming it. But this will not always be the case. There may be times when the MC will have to interact directly with the press during a "newsworthy" event. Unfortunately most "newsworthy" events in today's 24 hour news cycle are *negative news* events. Should this happen to your MC you will have to meet the press head-on to move forward the MC's story in the best light possible. One of the most direct ways to meet the press head on is to hold a press conference.

The Press Conference

A press conference is a meeting where press/media outlets are called together to cover a newsworthy event. A press conference can also be a cost-effective promotional tool for an MC because rides and events organized on a small budget can be boosted by the resulting news coverage. This is akin to free advertising!

Step 1
Decide the topic of the press conference. To be successful, the

topic or MC event should be newsworthy or of significant interest to the general public so that media outlets are more likely to send reporters to cover it. Though you should have press conferences to announce runs, charity events, parties and other topics; high-profile negative events like club shoot-outs, fights, murders, police harassment and other negative events will always drive the true media prurient interests to attend your press conferences. I say, get in the habit of holding press conferences for all of your good stuff, like annuals and parties, to get plenty of practice under your belt for that terrible day when the bad things happen and you have no choice but to have a press conference. Better to get used to press conferences when you have a friendly press with which to contend.

Step 2
Select a date, time and location for your press conference. If your press conference is about a positive event being thrown, like an MC flag football tournament, check your community calendar and chamber of commerce business calendar. Make sure the date you choose does not conflict with other significant or newsworthy events that might draw attention away from your press conference. For negative events it will not matter—they will be coming.

Step 3
Plan the press conference at least two weeks in advance. This will give you enough time to write a press release, gather a media kit, and determine appropriate media outlets to contact. Appropriate contacts are those organizations with an interest in covering topics related to MC styled events. For negative events worry not—the scheduling can surely be last minute.

Step 4
Distribute your press release to media contacts a week before the event. If you have existing professional relationships with reporters or news assignment editors, send your press release to their attention. Follow up the distribution with a personal phone call to assess interest in covering the event. Provide the reporter with background or inside information that will make it easier to cover

your press conference. For example, if your MC is building ten homes with the Habitat for Humanity group, provide the reporter with statistics that indicate the impact to the community your project will bring.

Step 5

Make advance arrangements for interested reporters to interview an MC VIP like the President, VP, or Founder before or after the conference. Setting a specific time will ensure the reporter attends the event. Large press conferences should include a media kit for each media outlet in attendance. The kit should include the MC's history, biographies of important members, appropriate photography for reprint and a copy of your press release. Though a PRO is a spokesperson, the press likes to talk to VIPs and decision makers. This makes them feel like they have an authoritative person to speak to who truly represents the organization. An interview from a President will always trump an interview with the VP or PRO. An interview from the PRO will always trump an interview with a Road Captain, and so forth.

Step 6

Stage the press conference area at least an hour before anyone is expected to arrive. Include a podium with your MC colors placard or a long table and chairs if more than one speaker will be participating. Set up seating for the expected number of attendees and test microphones, sound systems and lights if you have them. Make sure there are plenty of heavy duty extension cords so power is available. Pitchers of cool water, grapes or fruits are not expensive but show you know how to treat guests. This may go a long way in getting future press conferences covered.

Step 7

Appoint a Prospect to greet reporters as they arrive for the conference and to coordinate photo opportunities and interviews with company representatives.

Step 8

Begin the press conference at its appointed starting time by approaching the podium, welcoming attendees and introducing the main speaker or speakers. Speakers should be brief with remarks, highlight the key elements of the topic that the press conference is about, and then open the floor to questions.

Step 9

Control the questioning professionally. Do not allow it to become a free-for-all. Take charge and call upon the reporters per the raise their hands. Spread the questioning out equally. Do not allow one reporter to steal the show or guide the questioning to meet his/her agenda. If one reporter is hogging the time or really pressing forward a negative agenda, move the questioning to the other side of the room. Phrases like, "Let's call upon someone else who hasn't asked any questions today." is a good way to take charge. Gage your speaker's ability to continue the interview. If you see your President getting frustrated - call a pause or call the conference. This is YOUR show. You run it!

Step 10

End the press conference by having 'stepping up to the podium' signal the close of the conference, and thank attendees for coming. Make yourself and the speaker (for instance, the President) available after the press conference to verify information and answer follow-up questions.

Step 11

Send personal messages of thanks to media representatives covering your press conference the day after the event. This courtesy strengthens your media relations, which will be an asset in successfully planning future events.

**Not all press conferences are called to announce positive news. A press conference can also be a valuable tool for damage control in the event of an MC scandal, accident or incident that requires immediate public explanation. If you must plan this type of press conference, consider calling the conference by sending an electronic announcement to appropriate media outlets noting the time, date, and location of the event. Depending on the severity of the situation, it may be best for the press conference to consist only of the PRO (you) or the President reading a brief statement (prepared by you) and responding to a limited number of follow-up questions or no follow-up questions at all.

Case Study: Why Throw A Press Conference for Negative Events? Because the press will 'lie on you' if you don't

I was once watching a television news story in which a horde of bikers (mostly crotch-rockets) up near the New York area, got into a clash with an Asian family in an SUV. The resulting confrontation led to a young man being run over, on his motorcycle, and paralyzed while the Asian couple was being chased down by the horde of bikers. Ultimately, the Asian man (driver) was pulled from his SUV and subsequently beaten in front of his wife and child. The news coverage went berserk!! The horde of bikers were called a "biker gang", "thug bikers", and on and on. There was one MC that had a few members in vests that I saw in the footage but the rest seemed to all be independents.

Unfortunately, it seemed that the one MC that was there did seem (to me) to have some of its members participating in the beating of the driver. That would be a good time to call a press conference to get the MC's story to the forefront and start damage control. During that event motorcycle clubs all over the country, including some of the most hard core 1%ers were coming out with interviews and press releases disavowing the violence and clearly pointing out that the horde of bikers were not an organized MC or "biker gang."

◊◊◊

The Backgrounder

A Backgrounder is an informational document often provided with a press release, media alert, or as part of a larger media kit.

The backgrounder gives the press or other interested parties a more detailed background about an issue, event, person of interest, or launch. Knowing how to write a backgrounder is not a bad skill to possess. A backgrounder is provided because other press or media documents such as media alerts and press releases are necessarily kept short and succinct. The backgrounder provides more information to the journalist or media outlet without compromising the readability or standard format of the media alert or press release.

How to Write a Backgrounder

To write a backgrounder, begin with a short introduction to the topic at hand. Then, insert subtitles based on the additional information that you would like to provide the media. Some examples of common backgrounder subtitles or subsections are listed below. Last, fill in the information as appropriate under your subsections. Since most of your documents will be aimed at media organizations, write the backgrounder according to AP style. Keep in mind that you're writing for busy professionals, so make ample use of subheads and easy-to-reference graphics. Outside research should be heavily cited within the backgrounder, as journalists will often want to follow-up and verify your information.

Consider editing the backgrounder based on your targeted media outlet. Think about who your ideal media outlet is for the event you're working on. Then, consider if they'd be more interested in the history of your event, the roles of the people in the MC, or the geographical applicability of the MC's work at hand. Despite the above suggestions, backgrounders (like all pieces aimed at journalists) should be kept brief. The last thing you want to do is lose the interest of the media!

Parts of a Backgrounder

Typical sections of a backgrounder may include history of the MC, event or topic at hand, applicable statistics or other data; the names, descriptions, and qualifications of important people within the MC or event; direct statements about why the event or issue is applicable and worth covering in today's news cycle; geographical or population data related to the issue, and a few interesting items that the journalist could use to create their story.

How to Use a Backgrounder

Backgrounder documents may be used as part of a media kit-such as one stored on the MC's website or given out in hard copy during a press event. Note that this means it should render well in print and electronically.

They are often used in conjunction with press events, such as staged rallies or press conferences. Again, they are generally provided with several other documents as part of a media kit or press kit. They can be used in other ways too, such as a way to introduce a new chapter of the MC, issue or event to the media, or as a touch-base for talking points.

A Backgrounder by Any Other Name

Backgrounders may often be referred to by other terms. For example, they may be combined with or confused with a "fact sheet" Often used as part of a larger "media kit."

Sample Backgrounder

Constitutional Violations of Bikers in Georgia

Biker Watch Advocacy Group

Backgrounder

In the course of working toward our mission of stopping police harassment of bikers at "motorcycles-only safety stops", a coalition of motorcycle clubs and motorcycle rights groups have all noted strikingly similar accounts of violations and overreaching police authority on the part of the Stop these Stops Coalition; when responding to these so-called "safety stops".

Coalition members working with the affected motorcycle clubs and other independent bikers noticed this pattern and shared incidents which prompted further research. The current status of the research is a Freedom of Information Act (FOIA) request of materials related to the so called safety stops.

Covert Violations Gathering Mission Conducted by Stop These Stops Coalition

The Stop these Stops Coalition often monitors these police check points that are designed to harass bikers, to ensure biker's constitutional rights are not being violated. The Coalition has been hard at work since 1998. To date the Coalition has documented 12,475 violations that it has turned over to Biker Watch- a biker's watchdog group and lobbying organization whose attorneys have filed a class action lawsuit against the California Highway Patrol and the Department of Transportation. To force accountability in this situation, the Coalition began a covert operation to document these heightened incidents. A FOIA request was officially filed on November 21, 2016.

Merits of the Biker Watch Lawsuit Filed Against Department of California Highway Rovers

The FOIA request revealed that the California Highway Rovers had no authority to conduct these police stops and searches. Furthermore, management knew they were out of protocol from emails circulated within the department. The emails noted that the department was aware that it had exceeded the scope of its legal authority to conduct these stops, however, it continued to conduct these operations so that it could continue to benefit from the revenues derived from issued tickets that made up for the shortfall in the department's budget. Biker Watch subsequently filed a lawsuit on behalf of local area bikers and motorcycle clubs.

Violations and Consequences

Biker Watch's lawsuit claims that the Highway Rover's safety checks violate the constitutional rights of San Diego area bikers. In addition, the resulting searches, seizures, and citations issued at these safety stops cause discrimination against bikers. Biker Watch has vowed to bring an end to these violations on the Biker condition of San Diego area bikers.

These sickening stories were gathered by Biker Watch and confirmed by court documents referred to in its lawsuit against the California Highway Rovers:

1. Emir Phillips (35) was pulled over at a safety stop on January 15, 2012 and given a citation for loud pipes. Though no audio equipment was used to legally determine the decibel level, his pipes allegedly were above legal levels. His bike was impounded leaving him unable to get to his job which was 25 miles from his home. He consequently was fired from his job and unable to recover his bike from impound. His Harley Davidson was sold at auction on January 31, 2012. Court documents revealed that Highway Rover officers knew that they could not confiscate his motorbike without using a decibel meter to verify its loudness, but laughed as they did so anyway.

2. Watanabe Hiru Kamatsu (23) was pulled over at a safety stop March 09, 2010 and given a citation for an illegal helmet. His 2009 Ducati 779 was confiscated and he was issued a $1,500 fine. His motorcycle was consequently lost and never returned by the California Highway Rovers. Later, his motorcycle turned up in a sting outside of a Tiajuana, Mexico night club. The defendant claimed he bought it from a Highway Rover officer. Court documents show the officer admitted that he only issued the citation so that he could confiscate Kamutsu's Ducati and sell it.

Biker Watch's lawsuit seeks unspecified damages and compensation for emotional distress.

About Biker Watch Advocacy Group

Launched in 1887, Biker Watch is an advocacy group that has supported biker rights since the inception of the first motorcycle. Its mission is to "Help bikers ride, live, love, and enjoy the biking lifestyle on two wheels

rain sleet or snow! Baby we gonna always ride!"
   Biker Watch is managed by CEO JBII at jbii@bikerwatch.com

Can you identify the elements of this backgrounder letter? Can you distinguish the differences between a media alert, a press release, and a backgrounder? Do you know the reasons when one is used over the other? Can all three be sent for the same event? Yes! **Your mission:** Write a backgrounder for some issue related to your MC. Get another PRO or perhaps the Secretary in your MC to evaluate it and make recommendations on how you can make it better! Then, perhaps, submit one!

◊◊◊

The Backgrounder Meeting

The Backgrounder meeting is called like a press conference, but instead of announcing a newsworthy event, it is used to build relationships with a target audience. For example, you may hold a Backgrounder Meeting to:

- Educate the community about the merits of the MC
- Have a meeting with a local Sheriff who may have concerns about your MC coming into town
- Have a meeting with a dominant 1%er to inform them about your MC seeking a blessing in their territory
- Having a meeting with the press to give them information about the MC to counter rumors or clarify issues that may not have risen to a particular newsworthy event

◊◊◊

The Op-Ed

Op-eds are long opinion pieces that are often placed in a newspaper "opposite of the editorial" page (hence OPposite-EDitorial). These are about 600 words, longer than the Letters to the

Editor which are on the editorial page. Although not always, op-eds are usually written by someone of note such as a subject matter expert, or an organization- like the MC that has a stake in the issue. Even though they may be crafted by a PRO, a stronger subject matter expert writing credibly on the MC's point of view would more than likely be the President, VP, or National Officer. For an Op-ed you would probably help the President craft the piece that would carry his name as the expert speaking on behalf of the MC. As stated Op-eds give a position on the issue, but may also include elements such as personal stories, etc.

Your mission: Write an Op-Ed about an issue of great concern to your MC. Get another PRO or perhaps the Secretary in your MC to evaluate it and make recommendations on how you can make it better!

◊◊◊

The Bylined Article

A bylined article is an authored article that you can write for placement in a magazine, newspaper, or other publication. A bylined article is one of the most effective tools available for establishing credibility with a target audience because it showcases you as a thought leader in your field. In so doing, the article draws attention to the stature and strength of the MC and helps differentiate it from others. Bylined articles are also useful for drawing attention to issues important to the MC. For instance, an MC that is volunteering at retirement homes could write an article about the special skills needed to interact with elderly Jewish patients who were once interned in Nazi concentration camps. By-lined articles are long opinion pieces or news pieces. They are about six hundred to seven hundred fifty words. Longer than the Letters to the Editor which are on the editorial page, they can be written by someone of note such as a subject matter expert, or President who has a stake in the issue. They may also be crafted by the PRO for the President or National Officer.

Placing Your Article

Once you've decided a bylined article is a good PR strategy for your MC, the next step is identifying your target publications. Very often, finding target publications for your bylined article is as easy as flipping through your favorite motorcycle magazines and motorcycle websites. Once you've identified possible opportunities, call or e-mail the editor to confirm the writing policies, potential opportunities, and specifications for the article. Most publications will have a set of simple rules about what should and should not be included in an article. Word count, style, format, use of source materials, and attribution will all be spelled out. Often, you will find this information right in the masthead of the magazine or website. The vast majority of byline opportunities will stipulate that you not reference your MC or product in the article. Overt promotion is frowned upon and could result in your article being dismissed or severely edited. To avoid such penalties, it is best to err on the side of caution. For example, instead of inviting the readers to buy tickets to your party; write about the fun to be had, the trophies, the trophy walk, music, food, and the crazy Emcee. Write about the date of the annual and what time the party is typically held and voilà; you've done everything except ask someone to buy a ticket while still getting the message out that the event is something everyone need attend!

Writing the Article

Sometimes, before an editor accepts your pitch, he or she will likely ask you to submit an outline and a one-paragraph abstract summarizing your proposal. Even if such materials aren't required, it's good practice to prepare an outline before you get started. The subject of your article will be largely determined by the publication you're targeting. Some editors may even assign a specific topic. A common theme of bylined articles is proposing a problem and providing a solution. While you may not be able to directly cite your MC in the article, a well-written byline will present the reader with a problem and a recommended solution- a solution your MC just happens to provide.

Another favorite theme for bylined articles is the lesson learned. This approach involves using actual examples from you or your MC's history to illustrate instances of overcoming obstacles. The benefit of this style is that it lets you directly discuss your MC. However, the catch is that you must be candid about situations when you and your MC experienced difficulties, or perhaps failure. I often write about failures of the Mighty Black Sabbath MC Nation. It isn't always pleasant to acknowledge failure but the lessons learned part is always refreshing. Case studies that involve your members (with the member's permission) are also excellent for offering an impartial third-party viewpoint. An additional benefit of using a case study is that it will serve to further showcase expertise of your MC or leadership at handling a particular situation.

Promoting Your MC with Your Byline

In your byline, if the editor allows it, include your MC's web address and contact details. Make a note of when the article will be published and ensure you will be available to answer inquiries. Usually, once your article is published, it becomes the copyrighted material of the publication; so you must adhere to its copyright rules. However, you will likely have a chance to buy reprints. These can be used as part of a press kit. Some publications offer electronic versions for online posting.

So take the challenge. Write a bylined article! Though bylined articles take time and effort, the rewards of becoming a thought leader in the MC community can be immense. Soon, you will be ready to write your first MC book! Writing bylined articles is exactly how I got started, and they are part of what gave me the experience to write this book.

Writing a bylined article for the President

MCs had not traditionally thought to write bylined articles that directly affect PR until Hollywood started taking incredible liberties by stealing their names and making B-rated movies that depicted the MCs in the worst light possible. News agencies have also not been kind. Piggybacking off of the stereotypes created by the movie industry, lots of commercials and ads have been sold from news stories depicting salacious MC events with little regard for the facts of a story. Again, I am reminded of the amazing news stories that circulated in New York, not long ago, about a vicious motorcycle gang that attacked an Asian couple with their baby in the back seat. As discussed earlier, it turned out that the overwhelming majority of riders in that horde were independent and did not belong to any MC. Yet, not one retraction was ever printed. A young man that was crippled in the incident was portrayed as a thuggish member of the biker "gang" that never really existed. One of the biggest OMCs in the country decided to take their reputation back maybe thirty years or more ago. They began by hiring lawyers and copyrighting there colors, logos, and namesake. They stopped allowing Hollywood to make money off of them and took direct control of their PR. They jealously guard their reputation because positive public opinion is important. There was a time where MCs could sit on the sidelines and let whomever print whatever about them. Today's MC should be proactive about putting out stories, articles, information, and written pros portraying them in a positive light. There is much that affects the MC's brand with the 24/7 news cycle, Klout scores, and Twitter followers; all of these things factoring into the brand value equation. The more positive content you can contribute to the MC's PR effort- the better. You can also write bylined articles for senior leaders (such as the President) of your MC casting them as thought leaders and experts within the MC community.

Ghost Writer

The proper term is "Ghost Writer" and it is awesome job dedicated to making the person you are writing for look really great. Obviously, most Presidents are not going to be very great at writing cutting edge Op-Ed pieces or newsworthy articles. They have focused their careers on other things, for the most part, like growing and running MCs. Thus, the President has a weapon in his arsenal, and that weapon is you! The PRO is the professional communicator, guardian of the MC's reputation, and manager of its publics. There will be a natural division between the PRO and the President for who he/she is writing. The PRO will want to focus on the club's mission and the President will want to focus on himself. Despite this, as the PRO, you keep the writing focused on the MC's message. Fight the urge of the President to keep the focus on himself. Keep the expert bylined article to about six hundred words and follow these tips:

- **Manage Expectations Before You Start Writing:** Start with a clear outline that lays-out the headline theme, key data points, and desired outcomes.
- **Write for your Audience:** Your subject should address a desired audience's need. Stick to that mission.
- **Say it with data:** Consider the impact of these two lines: 1) Motorcycle clubs save lives when they have Road Captain training of their members. 2) An American Motor-biker's survey shows that motorcycle clubs that hold Road Captain education training have 72% fewer traffic accidents and 80% fewer traffic citations than motorcycle clubs that do not. The second sentence has the bigger impact because it has quantifiable statistics.
- Avoid MC Biker Set Jargon: If you use a word like

"properties" make sure to explain what it means. Write articles that anyone can understand.

- Keep secret things secret: You may learn a lot of things about the President that general members do not know, after working with him so closely. Keep your mouth shut about MC business or President business that you might glean. Protecting the President's image is your job as well.

Writing articles in conjunction with the President on a subject like motorcycle safety, fostering brotherhood/sisterhood, bonds and commitment, charitable giving, rides for humanity, motorcycle mechanics, and maintenance could bring your MC notability that could go a long way in the eyes of the public when times are hard. Consider finding publications that will accept contributions from an MC expert and start your President a column.

Case Study Ezine.com

Speaking of really trying your hand at writing bylined articles, I would suggest starting a membership with Ezine.com. An e-zine is a magazine (or newsletter) published only in electronic form on a computer network. E-zines are most commonly used to market products and sell something. E-zines are only sent to people who subscribe to them or are looking for the information they offer so the articles always get to welcoming eyeballs! Ezine.com is a place where you can do 'article-marketing'; which is a cool way to market your MC all over the world! Most people use it to market their products and sell their products by writing short articles (at least 200 words) about the benefits of some topic. It just so happens, that most of the folks who write about these benefits have a company that provides a product that will give you that benefit they are educating you about! Ezine.com will allow you to place a small link or reference to that product, but only one or two small references. They absolutely will not allow you to do naked advertising. The rest of the article has to be about solving a problem, or getting this benefit etc. The key is that the author builds his/her credibility as a subject matter expert and a thought leader about whatever subject. This builds trust with the reader, who may then want to buy your product, because they feel like you know what you are talking about. A reader who wants to know more about the subject or how to avail themselves of the benefit or solution may click on the link in the article and be taken to a website where they may obtain said product. Wow! "But what does that have to do with the MC," you may ask.

Well, I wanted to figure out how I could use the Ezine principle of article-marketing (selling products via creating author expertise and trust rather than outright advertising) to expose the Mighty Black Sabbath MC Nation to national and international audience in an effort to build chapters nationwide and worldwide. In 2009 I established an account as John E. Bunch II 'Author' and began writing articles about MC's and MC life. At that point NO ONE was writing about MCs (especially the Black Biker Set) at all, and certainly not using that vehicle to get their message out! So now, seven years later thousands and thousands of people around the world have read those articles that I wrote seven long years ago! One of my absolute great honors was that when I was criticized by that attack piece article that was written about me (I allude to in another place in this book) the author actually referenced those Ezine.com articles I wrote seven years ago! YES!!! Yes!!! Yes!!! Like we used to say on CB radios back in the day... "Good Buddy you are definitely gettin' out!"

The author of the attack piece said that he had run into my articles several years earlier and they had helped him form his hateful opinion of me! He actually quoted my articles directly and tore them apart nearly word for word!!! Then, he even put a link to one of my articles in his attack piece!!! YES!!! YES!!!! Yeeeeeessss!!! Now, even more folks could read my articles and make up their own opinions as to the relevance of my work. He sent me a blessing in disguise!

My Ezine.com articles established me, early in the game, as a thought leader in the MC subject matter arena. Remember that not everyone will agree with what you are writing. Some will actually take great issue to it. Fear not! If you are a good writer (or working to get better) controversy will only make you better. The Ezine.com articles also accomplished my mission of spreading the name of my beloved MC internationally. It is hard for me to quantify exactly how much the articles helped in our march across the United States, but most people who know of us know that we are a national MC with chapters spread from coast to coast. When people call me to ask if they can open BSMC chapters they always start with, "I've read so much about the MC online that I want to be 'A Breed Apart' with the Mighty Black Sabbath MC Nation."

So what did I write about? I wrote about things like, "How to Write Bylaws", "Freeloading at MC Annuals", "Starting a Motorcycle Club 101" and other MC related subject matter. In each article there was a link to a Black Sabbath MC website. Not all of my articles were all that great - heck, I was just getting started! I still had a lot to learn about the Set and MC protocol, and sure, I made some mistakes. I may have even written some things that were actually dead wrong. Even a surgeon kills a few patients before he perfects the game. At least with an article you can go back and make changes to update it later. The surgeon only gets one shot - but he keeps going until he is the greatest brain surgeon in the world! So that is what you must do! Though I have written for my Ezine.com account for a few years, whenever I go back there I still see people reading my articles just like I only wrote them yesterday.

I have committed myself to start writing Ezine.com articles again when I finish this book, to do the article-marketing necessary to sell this book. I'll take 200 words out of a chapter or two and write a solution to a MC PRO problem - say, like "Crisis Management." After reading how to solve the problem readers may want to know more from me as an author so they may click the link in my article and voilà they land on the website "PROsBible.com" where they can purchase my book and also learn about my MC! - Cool huh?

Your mission: Get busy writing bylined articles for the MC, the

President, and for yourself!

◊◊◊

The Letter to the Editor

The letter to the editor is usually a shorter opinion piece. It is written in letter format.

Sample Letter to the Editor

Dear Editor,

I'm writing to express my concern about the new height of speed bumps installed in the Pleasant Valley neighborhood of Mt. Hope. Though speed bumps are necessary to control unruly traffic in our neighborhoods, studies by the National Traffic Safety Institute have discovered that if they are over 6.3 inches high they represent a terrible hazard for motorcycles.

The Mighty Black Sabbath Motorcycle Club Nation joins the united forces of San Diego motorcycle clubs to ask the city to reconsider their decision to deploy two hundred 12" high speed bumps throughout the Mt. Hope area. We will be uniting at Qualcombe theater in July to protest this decision as we believe that biker lives should not be risked to promote public safety that doesn't protect the entire public—us! We believe that both goals can be accomplished. The city can have its speed bumps and we can be safe while traversing them.

The Environmental Study Association for Motorcycle Accident Survival has taken a position of support for area bikers and motorcycle clubs. They have 92 documented cases of severe to catastrophic injuries caused when bikers have tipped over traversing the 12" speed bumps versus almost zero injuries when they have fallen from the 6.3" speed bumps. We believe this is compelling evidence to cause the city to rethink their position. Finally, the cost savings in more than 1/2 as the smaller speed bumps are little more than half the price of the larger speed bumps.

I urge you to urge your readers to contact their City Council representatives and urge them to vote to use the 6.3" speed bumps! Please find contact information on the City Council's website.

Sincerely

James T. Kirk
Public Relations Officer
Mighty Black Sabbath Motorcycle Club Nation

Since 1974 and Still Strong
4280 Market Street San Diego, 91111
www.blacksabbathmc.com
PROJames@blacksabbathmc.com

Your Mission: Write a letter to the editor. Then bounce it off of someone whose opinion you trust to see how you can make it better.

◊◊◊

The Fact Sheet

The fact sheet is similar in function to the backgrounder, although may be less detailed, shorter, and less of a narrative than a set of facts relating to a story, organization, or event. Also, fact sheets are much more oriented to numbers, stats, and figures. Fact sheets are great as brochures!

Sample Fact Sheet
Mighty Black Sabbath MC Nation Black Out Party
Fact Sheet:
Location:
Seal Beach

Date:
XXXX

Time:
XXXX

Attendance:
Crowds range from 50,000 Bikers to 100,000 Bikers

Parking:
Tough/recommend taking trolley

Camping:
Available for dry camping RVs No Hookups

Entertainment:
22nd Street Biker Boyz
El the Barge
Janet Jacksonville
Too Shorty
The Artist formerly Known as Princess

Tickets:
$25 in advance TicketProfessionals.com
$52.66 at the door

Your mission: Write a Fact Sheet about an event that is happening within your MC. Get another PRO or perhaps the Secretary in your MC to evaluate it and make recommendations on how you can make it better!

◊◊◊

The Pitch Letter

A Pitch Letter is a brief letter, almost never longer than one page, written to accompany press releases, media alerts, or media kits. Pitch letters serve one purpose—to pique the journalist's interest in your story. They need not tell the whole story. Rather, they are "teasers" for the meat of your story angle. A pitch letter is formatted like a regular business letter.

The best way to learn how to write great pitch letters is to look at some that other folks have written, and then have a go of it on your own! I'll write some examples below. Before long, you will get the feel for the kind of style needed to write successful pitch letters.

In the first sentence, try to give the reporter something that will pique their interest to your angle of a story. Get straight to the point, and don't bury your angle in hyperbola.

Sample Pitch Letter:

March 1 2016

Mr. Thomas Franklin
Lifestyles Editor
The Daily Bugler
Manyplaces, GA 44444

Dear Joe

On November 21, on the outskirts of Atlanta, GA the Mighty Black Sabbath MC Nation will have the largest number of motorcycles ever seen in a continuous circle! In an attempt to shatter the Guinness Book of World Records' title held by the Silver Spokes of Satan MC the Black Sabbath MC will be going for it all!

The Black Sabbath will also be riding in various stunt formations and conducting acrobatics never before seen by an MC. The set will feature a high wire act, slow roll race, slow drag race, and a world championship sit still race where the first place will be $100,000 dollars! The contests will be open to all bikers.

Paul 'Pep' Perry founder of the Mighty Black Sabbath MC Nation will be available to discuss the history of the MC and the importance of breaking the world record; as well as his role as founder of the Black Sabbath Motorcycle Club Nation.

I'll be in touch soon to discuss a possible interview. Look forward to speaking with you.

Sincerely,

Trina 'Rolling Daisies" Rawlins
Public Relations Officer
RollingDaisiesPRO@blacksabbathmc.com

Here is another example - a pitch letter that informs the news editor of something they did not know.

Ms. Sophia Etherbacker

Features Editor
CyclePorn Magazine
Justanother City, Ga 2444

A cornucopia of abundance has risen from chaos and nutrition is being harvested where none was before.

What used to be a trash-filled vacant lot covered with hypodermic needles is now a 2 acre neighborhood garden in the plighted neighborhood of Mt. Hope in San Diego, California. Sitting on the fault line between two warring San Diego gangs, the Black Sabbath Motorcycle Club took the bold steps to take a lot that was once used to discard dead bodies, and turn it into a neighborhood garden to provide fresh vegetables for a community that has no stores within a 15 mile area that sells fresh vegetables.

The Black Sabbath MC and the children of Mt. Hope who have helped to build the beautiful garden have been given keys to the city by San Diego Mayor Julian B InCharge. The children of Mt. Hope were also given Green Thumb awards by Home Depot for their achievements as Jr. Farmers.

Sincerely,

Trina 'Rollling Daiseis" Rawlins
Public Relations Officer
RollingDaisiesPRO@blacksabbathmc.com

Target your pitch.
Even if you have only one version of a press release, you can still target your pitch to a particular media outlet by crafting a specific pitch letter. The purpose of the pitch letter in this case -- to frame the story in a way that makes it clear to the journalist that it fits in with that media outlet's approach.

Follow up your phone or e-mail pitches with a strong letter. Pitch letters are wonderful and often underused tools. Just keep them short, get to the point, try to show how your story can appeal to a wide audience where appropriate, have a little fun, and you'll be pitching like the PRO pros!

Can you identify the elements of this Pitch Letter?

Your mission: Write a Pitch Letter to pitch an event being hosted by your MC. Get another PRO or perhaps the Secretary in your MC to evaluate it and make recommendations on how you can make it better!

◊◊◊

The Media Kit

A Media Kit (also known as a Press Kit) is a package of several informational documents that is provided to the press and others to generate interest and news coverage. It is called a media kit because many times potential advertising mediums will ask for more information about a subject to be presented in a 'kit' format. The media kit may include any or all of the pieces listed on this page, along with FAQs, fact sheets, photos, brochures, graphics, biographies, press releases, etc. A press kit is meant to reach out to the press, and to introduce a big picture of someone or something; such as a controversy, issue, organization, or upcoming event.

Though media kits are often designed for specific events, you should have a general media kit about your MC always available to hand out. A press kit is like a resume for your MC. In it is a collection of MC information and articles put together to address questions from the media and others. The goal of the media kit is the same as all other marketing that a MC does. It should grab the reader's attention, make a lasting impression and create enough interest that they will contact you for more information.

Here are some ideas about what to include in your media kit. Of course, this is not a comprehensive list and is intended only to provide ideas for what is needed for your target audience:

1. **Pitch Letter:** Sometimes referred to as Letter of Introduction, this first impression item is where you will grab or lose the reader's interest. Tell them upfront why they should care about what you

are telling them. Provide a table of contents or a brief description of the items enclosed in the actual press kit. Let them know you are available for follow-up interviews and questions. Also, make sure to include your contact information in this letter.

2. **Information on the MC:** This includes your MC's history, a club profile, and profiles of the executive committee, VP, and President. Include bio sheets, if appropriate.

3. **Recent press publications and articles:** Copies of recent press coverage is very appropriate for a press kit. After all, what other media have done will be of interest to current media targets. This can include article reprints and printouts of online press that a company might have received.

5. **Press releases:** Many times, these are what instigated and caused the printing of the documents described above.

6. **Audio and video** files of radio or TV interviews, speeches, performances, and any other media-covered event: Hard copies will suffice if the actual media is not available.

7. **A sample news story:** This is your chance to guide the media or your reader. Some editors will even print it verbatim as they view ready-to-print articles as an easy way to fill up space with little effort on their part. They do, of course, usually edit these stories. So, be prepared.

8. **List of frequently asked questions:** This helps the editor determine what questions to ask you in an interview or what to include in the article. Some editors will even print this verbatim as well, which allows you to *ask and answer* the questions which is always a win-win scenario.

10. **Other items to include:**
   - Nonprofit and community-service involvement
   - Recent awards

- Photos (if appropriate)
- Factual background material and/or white papers
- Specific information and schedules of upcoming promotions and events
- Significant statistics specific to your industry, demographics and target audiences
- Feature article material, such as articles written by company officers or senior management
- Missions, goals, and objectives
- Camera-ready logo art
- Giveaway information

The Key to Getting Noticed

Busy editors sort through piles of media kits each day. Getting your media kit noticed is the key to publication and action! Remember, getting attention is important not only with audiences, but also with editors. Package your materials in a unique way and make sure the materials are presented professionally. It is also crucial to follow up to make sure your intended recipient received your Media kit. Plus, follow-up calls provide the perfect opportunity for editors to ask questions or schedule an interview. Use this opportunity to build relationships with editors--in fact, doing so will improve your chances of publication or acceptance by your intended audience. Because the distribution of media kits can get a little expensive, you have got to make relationship-building a part of your marketing strategy. You can also have your media kit completely digital on a CD.

Your mission: Start assembling part of your media kit, based on available materials. Then, add to it as you see fit and develop new materials. You do not want to create a media kit at the last minute. Typically, the media kit doesn't have to be as fancy as people think. Those requesting media kits just want information--not necessarily glitz. See what items you already have and then work on the rest.

The Columnist

It is entirely possible that a PRO representing an MC is provided a recurring column in a media publication. Often this is a nod to the MC's depth of knowledge on MC subject matter that has a wealth of different viewpoints and news items to write about. Consider, for example, an MC dedicated to eradicating poverty through feeding the hungry/homeless in city parks on the weekend. The MC's PRO or President may be granted an ongoing column in which to discuss general developments in the area.

Your Mission: See if you can get published!
◊◊◊

The Media List

A Media List is the list or "Black Book" or "Rolodex" that you have comprised of media, law enforcement and other important contacts. There is a saying, "You're only as good as your list" so creating media lists that work is important. The best strategy, development, and writing mean absolutely nothing if they don't land in the right hands. Media lists are the most important tool in a media relations arsenal and often they do not get the time and attention they deserve. Take time up front to save a lot of time down the road. Grow your media contacts and cultivate your relationships. Provide your media folks with good information and they will come to you time after time.

Here are some top tips for developing media lists:

- Check and recheck: Once you have a start on the list, it is your job to make it work for you. Call media outlets to make sure your contacts are still there and covering the same beat.
- Check online to see if your contact reports about what you think they do.

- Ensure that your list notes include any information you have gathered along the way, such as the best way to approach reporters, what days/time they work, etc.
- Spell it right: Nothing is a bigger turn-off to the media than seeing their name spelled wrong. If it sounds like a tricky one, note the phonetic spelling in the notes section.
- Include: Name, email, phone, fax, snail mail, details of all past interactions with the reporter, and previous stories relating to your client or their industry.

Your mission: Start developing your media list using the strategies mentioned above.

◊◊◊

Talking Points

Have you ever watched a television interview of a politician where the reporter will ask a question but the politician never seems to answer it?

Reporter: "So sir, why exactly did you vote for the "Death to all motorcycle clubs" bill?"
Politician: "The important thing Connie, is that all motorcyclist should realize that they are welcome in the city if they ride safely and obey our traffic laws—MC's included, this weekend but inappropriate behaviors will not be tolerated from anyone!"

You are sitting there in front of the television thinking, "Hmmmm, that didn't seem to be the answer to the question, is it me? Am I retarded? That politician just answered the question without an answer yet kept on talking like it was ok!"

It is likely that the politician was speaking from his "Talking Points" which are never really designed to answer questions in the first place, but rather to get the point across he wants to deliver and not let the reporter's bias take him off message or cause distractions. One fear people have when they know they are going to be speaking in public, giving interviews- or worse, when they are pounced upon by a hostile reporter with an impromptu interview— is that when "they" come for you, perhaps you will not be able think of anything to say! Thus, having talking points committed to memory, on a 3X5 card, smart phone, tablet, or a tele-prompter can save the day! It is not enough to plan a meeting to talk about keeping your clubhouse from being shut down with the city attorney (this happened to the Black Sabbath in 1999), policymakers, bureaucrats, or the media. You must to have something to say when you get to the meeting! Astute PROs send their Presidents and officers to meetings and interviews armed with a secret weapon: talking points!

Talking points are a short list of arguments in support of a particular position; a set of remarks which are carefully planned and written down before a meeting, speech, or interview. Effective talking points organize and focus your thoughts so they will deliver your arguments effectively and concisely. They can also keep you from being lost or sidetracked from your message. Meetings with strangers, VIPs, reporters, law enforcement, and dignitaries can be unnerving. With good talking points in your hand (in your President's hand) or committed to memory, you will be confident and better prepared to deliver your message successfully.

Talking points can be developed for just a single meeting or can be ongoing, working to define a MC's mission statement or direction. For example, you may give all officers, members, and prospects in your MC a set of talking points that they could use when talking to anyone; during recruiting or just sitting around talking about the MC like this:

1. *The Mighty Black Sabbath Motorcycle Club Nation was established in 1974 by seven black men who rode on Sundays.*
2. *The original seven founding fathers used to meet in each other's garages every other Sunday until one day, the wives revolted and shut down their garage access.*

3. Undaunted, the founding fathers acquired a clubhouse at 4280 Market street in San Diego, California and called themselves Black Sabbath MC; where they remained for 40 years.
4. Today the Mighty Black Sabbath Motorcycle Club Nation accepts all races, religions, creeds, and occupations
5. We are a non-violent MC with chapters nationwide devoted to riding motorcycles, big distances, rain, sleet, or snow!
6. We are also dedicated to giving back to the community through our dozens of charities nationwide.

As you can see, this is a small bullet list of six talking points that should be fairly easy for any member to remember at least three or four of them! Now let us test them out against an aggressive reporter who just so happened to catch one of your members in front of the MC—who was not necessarily authorized to speak for the MC but did so anyone because he was caught off guard, and fortunately he had committed the MC's talking points to memory:

Aggressive Reporter: "Is it true that you are an all-black MC that treats women poorly?"

Member: "Though the Mighty Black Sabbath Motorcycle Club Nation was established in 1974 by seven black men who rode on Sundays; today the Mighty Black Sabbath Motorcycle Club Nation accepts all races, religions, creeds, and occupations."

Aggressive Reporter: "Yeah, but do you treat women poorly? We have reports that you treat women poorly."

Member: "We are a non-violent MC with chapters nationwide devoted to riding motorcycles, big distances, rain, sleet, or snow! We don't treat anyone poorly."

Aggressive Reporter: "We've heard that you are a cult. With a name like Black Sabbath you must admit that you sound like a cult. Are you a cult?"

Member: "The Mighty Black Sabbath Motorcycle Club Nation was established in 1974 by seven black men who rode on Sundays. The original seven founding fathers used to meet in each other's garages every other Sunday until one day the wives revolted and shut down their access to the garages. Undaunted, the founding fathers acquired a clubhouse at 4280 market street and named themselves Black Sabbath MC because they were black men who rode on Sundays. They remained at 4280 Market Street for 40 years. For most of those 40 years, we were the only MC in San Diego to have a club house. Though we are proud and traditional we are not a cult."

Aggressive Reporter: Black men who rode on Sundays? So you are a segregated MC then?"

Member: "Today the Mighty Black Sabbath Motorcycle Club Nation accepts all races, religions, creeds, and occupations."

Aggressive Reporter: "What do you think about the war that's been reported between the two 1%er clubs in the region where four members of club A were shot and killed last week? Do you support club A or club B in the war?"

Member: We are a non-violent MC with chapters nationwide. Our energies are devoted to riding motorcycles, big distances, rain, sleet, or snow!"

Aggressive Reporter: I'm asking you what your opinion is about the 1%er war. Are your folks on the side of club A or club B? What advice would you give those two clubs if you were asked?

Member: The Mighty Black Sabbath Motorcycle Club Nation is also dedicated to giving back to the community through our dozens of charities nationwide. Would you like me to tell you about our charities?"

As you can see the reporter clearly has an agenda designed to shine the MC with a negative light. And it is a good thing to know that most reporters want to discredit the MC whenever you talk to them. There is a dynamic behind this phenomenon that is not personal but is good to understand. Contrary to popular belief, news agencies do not exist to edify the public and serve to better inform, educate, or even to necessarily tell them the truth. Rather, news agencies exist to sell papers, commercials and advertisement space. They have to continually generate newsworthy events to gain the eyeballs of information weary consumers. Often running with a common stereotype serves them much better than telling the truth, (more on this later) so reporters become adept at asking questions designed to back you in a corner and make the MC look like a stereotypical gang! DO NOT FALL FOR IT! Make sure your people have strong talking points when dealing with the press, law enforcement, or other agencies so they communicate the agenda of the MC and not the other way around.

Writing effective talking points is easy if you remember the following helpful guidelines:

- Define your main message. Perhaps the main message in the talking points above is contained in points four, five, and six. Ask yourself why are you meeting in the first place? What are you trying to accomplish after your message is delivered? Once you know why you are meeting, the rest of the talking points may easily fall into place.
- Keep your talking points short and sweet. Think bulleted lists, rather than novels. Instead of writing hundreds of points which may confuse or bore your listener; come up with no more than four or five main points which support your case. Then, develop those points with supporting arguments or evidence. Ideally, the whole thing should take no more than a page or less.

For instance, if your President wanted to talk to the state legislature about why they should stop harassing bikers at motorcycle-only "safety-stops", you may write his main talking points to look something like this:

I am against unnecessary and burdensome traffic stops on bikers at so called "motorcycle-only safety stops" because:

1. *As MC riders we are professionals, we have dedicated Road Captains who are duty bound by our bylaws to ensure every member of the MC rides safely in the pack.*
2. *Having our American made V-Twin motorcycles sitting in long lines idling in hot summer weather while we are waiting our turn to be searched causes expensive mechanical break downs.*
3. *The fourth amendment guarantees us protection against unreasonable or illegal search and seizure. To pull us over and not cars and trucks is blatantly biased and therefore unreasonable.*
4. *Finally, all bikers in the MC coalition in this area have subsequently taken rider safety courses so that these actions by*

law enforcement are no longer necessary.

Then you would list examples and arguments to back up each point. In this case, you would give specific examples of club bylaws that required the Road Captain to check the bikes for safety and so on.

Put your best foot forward. Write down all your talking points, and organize them so that the strongest ones are presented first and most persuasively. Stick to the point. Only use arguments which directly support your case. Get rid of any arguments or supporting evidence that do not fit. Avoid bringing up other issues which are not related to the safety stop searches or are not related to this particular situation. Provide specific examples that support your argument. Give concrete examples of how this problem is affecting the MC or the biker community; or how the MC or the biker community would benefit from your solution. Anecdotes about people in your MC or MC community who are personally affected by this problem are also often very effective.

Keep your remarks professional. Talking points are not an appropriate venue for calling names, naming names, or affixing blame. Stick to the facts and try to keep your comments neutral. For instance, saying "You rotten pigs are pulling us over for no damned reason except to harass us because you don't like motorcycle clubs in this area, you chicken sh*t mothaf**k**s" is not likely to advance your cause—even if it were all true! Focus your bikers on making statements in calm, thoughtful tones to evoke empathy, understanding, and win listeners over to their side.

Emphasize win-win solutions. Show how your solutions will benefit the state. Instead of them spending overtime money to police bikers in the area talking point number four gives them an out that does not violate their dignity and allows them to say mission accomplished while still shutting the program down. Win-win solutions are always more likely to be acceptable to your audience, and more likely to be implemented.

Your mission: Practice writing some talking points for a local issue that concerns your MC. Use the above guidelines to get started. Once you have written your arguments, organize them so that the strongest ones are presented first. Share what you have written with a fellow PRO or the Secretary in your chapter and get feedback on how your talking points can be improved.

CHAPTER FIVE
PR Tips

More Interview Tips

Use these interview tips or put them on a queue card for someone in your MC that is going to be interviewed:

- Keep your cool
- Do not be arrogant or hostile
- Do not be a robot. You can repeat for clarity.
- K.I.S.S. (keep it simple & stupid). Keep examples, ideas and stories simple.
- Do not give away too much. Say what you have planned to say then STOP!
- It is okay to take a "time-out" and pause. It is your interview.
- Use blocking and bridging (B&B) to get from the question to your message
- Use talking points
- If you do not know, do not speculate!
- Never repeat a negative
- You can start or stop an interview anytime!
- There is no perfect interview. When reviewing the interview do not be too hard on the interviewee.

- Monitor the coverage and learn closely from each experience

Your mission: If you know your President is going to have a tough interview—practice throwing tough questions at him/her!
◊◊◊
Article Writing Tips
When writing articles for the MC try using some of these tips:

- Think like the audience
- Imagine what concerns the audience, and come up with a solution to the problem
- Consider swaying minds instead of arguing to closed minds
- You catch more flies with honey than with vinegar
- Do not write accusations you cannot prove
- Do not spread rumors
- Never lie
- Stick to the facts unless writing Op-Eds
- Less is more
- Write several articles with fewer points than one large article with too many points
◊◊◊
What Makes News
Always be aware of what makes news so that you can be in front of it, break news, or combat negative news against your MC:

- Controversy
- Change
  - ○ new
  - ○ unique
  - ○ unusual
- Violence
- Natural disaster
- Charity work

- David facing Goliath (the MC vs. the city)
- Warm and fuzzy stories (MC visiting children with cancer)
- MC Wars
- Accidents, death, and injuries

◊◊◊

Relevance as a Tool

Relevance can be a tool you can use to link your MC to happening trends that can aid the MC. For instance, if the neighborhood was moving to save historical buildings from being torn down and transformed into high-priced condos; you might be able to get the local community board to get your forty-two year old motorcycle club listed as a traditional, historical site that cannot be demolished (this actually happened with a BSMC clubhouse).

How to find relevant matters:

- News stories can give you tips
- Link to an emerging trend
  - Use Stats
  - Leverage pop culture: New Biker Boyz movie release
- Timeliness
  - Event happening on the weekend (TV/daily/weekly newspapers)
  - Event in two or three months (local magazine/monthlies)
- Link to a local angle
  - Reporters always want local personal stories

◊◊◊

PR Plan Development
Here is an example of a PR Plan that you could employ for an MC event:

Develop Key message	6 months out
Write Press Releases • Social media • MC chat groups • websites • advertising	3 months out
E-mail and call local monthly pubs	3 months out
Email and call local daily newspapers • Features Editors • Special Interest Editors • Social media • MC chat groups • websites • advertising	2 months out
Call all local TV stations • News directors • News desk • Reporters • Social media • MC chat groups • websites • advertising	2 week out (call day of event to confirm attendance
Post event • Social media • MC chat groups • websites	Email "thanks" to all who covered event
Event debrief	Review coverage and process lessons learned

◊◊◊

What PR Do You Need

Can PR help your MC? That is only a question that can be answered by the Full Patch members of your MC. Ask yourselves:

- What is the mission of our MC?
- Are there any misconceptions in the public about our MC that can affect our mission or stop us from accomplishing our goals?
- What audiences are most important to us?
  - ○ Members?
  - ○ General public?
  - ○ Biker Set MCs?
  - ○ Special interest groups?
  - ○ Government officials?
- What is the message of the MC?

CHAPTER SIX
Use Media Coverage to
Document MC's History

Winners

It is said that history is written by the winners and perhaps that is true. For instance today's history books are being rewritten to say that African Americans arrived in this country to work as servants and barely even mention slavery. What do parents do about it? Do they write their own history books and educate their children with the truth? They could. But instead most sit by and do nothing as the past lessons of a noble people are eroded away. Maybe the saying should be, "History is written by those who are not so apathetic as to sit by and watch their history be written away!" Winning and losing really does not have much to do with it.

I find MCs are much the same in their apathy to document their own history. Have you ever heard of the San Diego, California Cobras MC, or the Wichita, Kansas Penguins MC? What about the San Diego Highway Kings MC, have you ever heard of them? Do you know who started them and where their club houses were? There may be tens of thousands of other MCs of which we could say, came, existed, rode, lived, loved, cried, laughed, died and contributed to the legacy of the mighty MC Nations lifestyle; then went the way of the Doe Doe bird. Extinct. They disappeared from the face of the Earth with no one except the old timers to even barely remember who they were. Perfect example, I think I remember an MC in San Diego named Limited Choice MC. My memory is so foggy about that MC, but I could swear there was an MC there by that name. I wonder if this will be the only book to ever mention their name. So, at some point I began to write and document MC history, and I encourage you to do the same; but I will tell you it will not always be easy or well received...

◊◊◊

Biker Boyz Aficionado

I take a lot of flak from many critics on the Biker Set who seem to be angry about my writings and public works, especially for my role in making the DreamWorks movie "*Biker Boyz*." In one attack piece a writer recently wrote of my book "Prospect's Bible"—the reason why no one should read the book was that I was generally a traitor to the so called *purity* of the Biker Set, and that *really* my "only claim to fame" was that of being a "Biker Boyz aficionado."

He argued that somehow I was some kind of fake/traitor that only had to offer my *meager* role as having been a Technical Advisor who "failed" as a prospect—therefore "*Prospect's Bible*" could not possibly contain any information of significance—as I was unqualified to write it! I suppose this was because I did not see things quite the way that he did (that will always spark an attack since people are never allowed to have their own opinions on the Biker Set), and one of my chapters had decided to throw a Beauty Pageant charity event. For those reasons, he attacked my book that he admittedly never read! All of this from a person I never once met, held a conversation with, never crossed, and never shared a harsh word. Wow.

The reason I tell you this story is to let you know that when you take a leadership role in documenting, writing, and publishing the MC's history—you may run into fierce resistance! When you expose yourself and your work to public scrutiny and muster the **audacity** to, among other things, stand up and document the history and contributions, to this lifestyle, of bikers on our Set—be prepared for some bumpy roads. People, on their own agendas, may write lies about you, may attack your integrity, and may be unfair to you. Still, the history of your MC is in your hands. You can write books, lectures, histories, blogs and informative reviews that will illuminate the qualities of the great peoples of your MC. I have sought to do this with my books. Not just to educate people by relating my experiences, but also to document the great history of the proud and noble peoples of the Mighty Black Sabbath MC Nation. You should do the same. Jump start yourself into making sure your folks are never forgotten!

I can also tell you that the beginning of what eventually became a movie and two books did not begin as some kind of noble cause. I did not wake up one day and decide that I needed to get busy protecting my MC's history. Actually, it began from frustration. It all started off quite innocently as just some regular guy watching a television show...

◊◊◊

Wild Ride of the Outlaw Biker

I must have been so excited when the documentary "*Wild Ride of the Outlaw Biker*" came on television sometime in the late nineties. I had my popcorn and juice and I just could not wait until the show got started. But so disappointed was I when this supposed "tell all" outlaw biker documentary was on, and as an entire hour had passed by, had not once mentioned a black motorcycle club yet! I felt like I was absolutely devastated. Then it replayed an old radio broadcast and that announcer mentioned the name of the East Bay Dragons when he was giving the rundown of outlaw clubs in the Oakland area, but other than that, no further mention of black bikers occurred in that show whatsoever. I felt just empty and disappointed. Nothing of substance about the contribution of African American bike clubs to the biker lifestyle, outlaw lifestyle or

MC lifestyle. I felt marginalized, empty and worthless because THEY did not say anything about US. Then my mind started wondering… they, they…, THEY!!! Who are they? Why am I always worried about they, them, and those!? It dawned on me- why should I wait on THEM to write about US when I am fully capable of writing history, interviews, books, magazines and yes, even movies about US all on my own!? I can write about US, We, OURS, MINE! What I could write would be as good as anything anybody else could write who would seek to exclude my history because they were biased or simply not interested in telling the whole story—or rather, my part of the story!

It was that night that I looked around my motorcycle club and noticed that all of the pictures of pretty, half-naked girls on the walls of the clubhouse were not of women who looked like our women but rather women who looked like others' women. It was like our women had no beauty and were not worthy to be posed up against the motorcycle. Our women were not on many of the Sports Illustrated Swim Suit covers, in the motorcycle magazines or in the biker movies. I awoke that night with a new determination to write the narrative of my own biker experience and began to use my advanced photography skills to publish my own biker magazine "Black Iron Motorcycle Magazine" and "Urban Biker" motorcycle magazine. Eventually, I found myself on the set of a movie, and of course, eventually labeled a Biker Boyz aficionado.

◊◊◊

Clifford Vaghs and Ben Hardy

After I was a grown man, clearly a motorcycle NUT, had long opined over the movie Easy Rider (one of the greatest motorcycle movies ever written), had day dreamed and loved the 'Captain America' motorcycle, after I had been a member of the Mighty Black Sabbath MC Nation for over a decade, had published my own motorcycle magazine, and even long after I had participated in making the Biker Boyz movie that featured a "Captain America" replica from the movie Easy Rider; did I ever once hear- that a black man named Clifford Vaughs designed the bikes for the movie; and actually gave one of the greatest biker movies of all times its name—"Easy Rider"! When I learned of this, I could not believe it. I had just come up with another reason to write my own history books. I had to play my part in ensuring that our contributions to history are never forgotten.

The story behind the Easy Rider choppers reveals two African-American bike builders: Clifford "Sonny" Vaughs, who designed the bikes, and Ben Hardy, a prominent chopper-builder in Los Angeles, who worked on their construction. Clifford Vaughs. In an article written on http://www.npr.org/2014/10/11/354875096/behind-the-motorcycles-in-easy-rider-a-long-obscured-story, NPR said Vaughs, believed Easy Rider conspicuously omitted the contributions of African-Americans to motorcycle culture. The article further claimed, "In fact, two documentaries about the production of Easy Rider — 1995's Born To Be Wild and 1999's Easy Rider: Shaking The Cage — never named the men who designed and built the choppers.

In an excerpt from the article called Raw Feelings Vaughs said he and others were fired and replaced early on in the film's production, following the chaotic shoot at Mardi Gras in New Orleans. As a result, his name never appears in the credits. While the film went on to become one of the top-grossing films of 1969 and a cultural touchstone, the name Clifford Vaughs has remained largely unknown. Vaughs said he has never watched Easy Rider, despite the fact that he designed the bikes used in the film. "I'm a little miffed about this, but there's nothing I can do," Vaughs says of the story, though he makes sure to note that he only spent about a month working on Easy Rider, out of a "long and illustrious life." He also said the absence of black characters in the film was troubling. In the 1960s, Vaughs belonged to an integrated motorcycle club known as The Chosen Few. That multi-ethnic reality was not reflected on screen. "Why is it that we have a film about America and there are no Negroes?" he asked. Vaughs says the omission of his own name and that of other African-Americans in the retelling of the Easy Rider story was conspicuous. "Those bikes, when we talk about iconic, they are definitely iconic," he said. "But yet, the participation of blacks ... completely suppressed, completely suppressed. And I say suppressed, because no one talks about it." Vaughs has never watched Easy Rider. When asked why, he responds simply, "What for?"

A blog site called "The Vintagent" (http://thevintagent.blogspot.com/2012/01/uneasy-rider-cliff-vaughs-story.html) chronicled Cliff Vaughs other contributions to the civil rights struggle of the 1960's. The article said, "Credit for the design of the 'Easy Rider' bikes (and other important aspects of the film, including the title!) goes to Cliff Vaughs, a civil rights activist, filmmaker, and biker (in the Chosen Few MC - a racially integrated club since 1960). Vaughs was a member of the SNCC (Student Nonviolent Coordinating Committee), a direct-action civil rights group. He was a figure in many of the famous sit-ins, freedom rides, and marches in the 1960s south. He participated in, and photographed, many of the legendary civil rights confrontations of the era; although he missed the March on Washington because he was "building a chopper" in his backyard. Vaughs was also a documentary film maker and made "What Will the Harvest Be?" about the rise of Black Power in the South. It included interviews with Martin Luther King, Stokeley Carmichael, and Julian Bond. It was aired on ABC-tv in the mid-60s. From documentaries, he moved into film production by the late 1960s. He was, also, clearly a motorcycle nut; and considered Ben Hardy his mentor in building, maintaining, and riding his machines.

After learning about stories like these, I knew I had to participate in anything public that would document, for posterity and generations of children to come, the histories and contributions of a noble and proud people.

◊◊◊

Why Wikipedia Doesn't Know You

I used to think Wikipedia was some fly by night wannabe online encyclopedia until I tried to put an article in it. Then I found out the real deal!

A few years ago I wanted to do some research on MCs so I launched Google and got to looking. Somewhere in my search I found Wikipedia and was astonished to find that the only information I could really find about MCs was mostly written about 1%er outlaw motorcycle gangs (OMGs). But there was really nothing written about 99%ers so I figured I would include my MC on Wikipedia (The Mighty Black Sabbath Motorcycle Club Nation) and let folks get to know us. I opened an account and started writing. That is when I learned some very interesting, if not disturbing, things about the entire Wikipedia process and why it is very possible that the historical recorders of mankind's knowledge will most likely never know your MC or our contributions to the Biker Set culture.

Wikipedia is a free online encyclopedia, written collaboratively by people who use it. It is a special type of website designed to make collaboration easy by allowing authors to contribute to a wiki-page. Because it is a collaborative effort, anything you post on Wikipedia may be changed, deleted or altered by someone else who is contributing to the "collaborative" effort. The tenant of Wikipedia, as established by its creators, Jimmy Wales and Larry Sanger, of the concept of free-as-in-freedom online encyclopedia. According to Alexa Internet, Wikipedia is the world's seventh-most-popular website in terms of overall visitor traffic. Wikipedia's total worldwide monthly readership is approximately 495 million. Worldwide in August 2015, WMF Labs tallied 18 billion page views for the month. According to comScore, Wikipedia receives over 117 million monthly unique visitors from the United States alone (https://en.wikipedia.org/wiki/History_of_Wikipedia).

So as you can imagine from the stats above that putting your MC on Wikipedia might be just a pretty big deal and give it exposure all around the world except for a few simple things; it is not that easy!!! You see Wikipedia does not allow any unverified information on the site and it has, what I call, Wikipedia trolls that hover all over the pages in their areas of "EXPERTISE" screwing up your articles and deleting whatever it is that they may not like. Better yet, they delete what may not be according to the very strict Wikipedia standards. In my case, they deleted every single positive thing I ever wrote about the Mighty Black Sabbath MC Nation. It was absolutely CRAZY! You had these so called Motorcycle Club 'expert', nerd-weenies who went through my Wikipedia post (which took over one month to write in the first place). You have to damn near write code to understand how to write a wiki article—I mean it is *intense!* They took out everything that was not be verified by an independent, outside, third party. You may ask, "Well, what does that mean?" And I would have to tell you it means this...

Wikipedia wants sources when you write something. So, if you say, "The Mighty Black Sabbath MC Nation was born in San Diego, California in 1974 at 4280 Market Street in a neighborhood called Mt. Hope." Wikipedia wants some kind of independent verification (SOURCE) that can verify your statement. If you do not have said source, they will give you an opportunity to get one—because one of these monitor weenies will leave a message saying something like "citation needed." After a while, you will come back and that statement will be gone, gone, gone.

So, if you wrote, "We have built homes for veterans, fed the homeless, go out every second Sunday and play bingo at the local retirement home, cut old folks yards, and ride motorcycles from coast to coast in the middle of the winter; no matter what—rain, sleet or snow-baby we gonna always ride" but all that anyone else, like news agencies and newspapers have ever written about you is the time someone got killed outside of your clubhouse or the time your clubhouse got shut down; then that will be the only thing left in your article. When dealing with a biased media that seems out to destroy the credibility of MCs at every turn it is easy to see why Wikipedia has you looking terrible or just does not know you at all. Because most MC's do not ever have anything positive written about them and a lot of the reason for this is that the PRO is not fighting hard for positive news coverage for everything positive that the MC does!

◊◊◊

Historical Documentation

From the stories I have told you in this chapter, I hope that I have convinced you of the importance the role the PRO has in documenting the MC's history. When outside interests, such as the media or Hollywood, write about the history of the MC; they control of the depiction of MC- not *we the People* of the MC. The media is biased towards the MC. It sells more advertisements, papers, magazines, and TV commercials when they can hook a viewing public on our mystique and supposed anti-social and negative behaviors, dehumanize us; and package us as thugs, outlaws, demons, and criminals. When I was a Technical Adviser for the DreamWorks movie "Biker Boyz" it was my utmost pleasure to create, in the lead characters, a club member that was a lawyer. It was a pleasure to guide set designers to creating the most lavish motorcycle clubs houses you had ever seen. That was because my reality was MC Club houses that were off the chain as I grew up on the Set from coast to coast. Like the East Bay Dragons' club house in Oakland, or the Cycle Kings mother chapter club house in Trenton, or the Front Runners' first mother chapter club house in Atlanta, or the Purple House (Regulators MC) mother chapter in Atlanta, or the Born Losers MC mother chapter Atlanta, Strikers MC club house in Atlanta, Second to None (Tulsa), the Mighty Black Sabbath MC Nation Club Houses in San Diego, Atlanta, Phoenix, Wichita, Macon & Little Rock, and on and on! If I was going to tell folks about the Biker Set- I was going to tell them about all of the great things we do and about our rich history and contributions to this culture. If our story is given over to outsiders to tell it is highly unlikely that the true story of our MCs will ever be told! I have often been criticized for participating in the first team to bring to the silver screen the African American point of view of the biking culture. Nevertheless, I am proud to have done so. I was proud to show our dignity and humanity in film to be recorded for all human existence (hopefully).

Therefore, I argue to you, that it is wise that the story of your MC should be written and produced by YOU in order for the story to remain in such a condition that it benefits the MC and represents the MC as the members would desire. As PRO you are most likely the best writer in the MC. Use your talents to endure the historical presence of the MC. Let the history of the MC be written by the winner. Insist that winner is you. When will there by another African American motorcycle movie written that was bigger and better than Biker Boyz? When you write it!

CHAPTER SEVEN
The Flyer

Definition and History of the Flyer

I could not wait to write this chapter because I get to talk about some of the stuff MCs do on flyer design that really crack me up! So let us get started. What is the purpose of a flyer?

Wikipedia defines a flyer as:

A flyer is a form of paper advertisement intended for wide distribution and typically posted or distributed in a public place, handed out to individuals or sent through the mail. In the 2010s, flyers range from inexpensively photocopied leaflets to expensive, glossy, full-color circulars. In the 2010s, electronic flyers are sent via e-mail. A flyer is also called a "flyer", "circular", "handbill", "pamphlet", "poster" or "leaflet". (https://en.wikipedia.org/wiki/Flyer_(pamphlet)).

Usage:

Flyers may be used by individuals, businesses, not-for-profit organizations, [MCs] or governments to:

- Advertise an event such as a music concert, nightclub

appearance, festival, or political rally

- Promote a goods-selling businesses such as a used car lot, discount store, or a service business such as a restaurant or massage parlor
- Persuade people about a social, religious, or political message, as in evangelism or political campaign activities on behalf of a political party or candidate during an election
- Flyers have been used in armed conflict: for example, airborne leaflet propaganda has been a tactic of psychological warfare.
- Recruit members for organizations or companies [or MCs].

Like postcards, pamphlets, and small posters; flyers are a low-cost form of mass marketing or communication. There are many different flyer formats. Some examples are:

A4 (roughly letterhead size)
A5 (roughly half letterhead size)
DL (compliments slip size)
A6 (postcard size)

Flyers are inexpensive to produce and they required only a basic printing press from the 18th century to the 20th century. Their widespread use intensified in the 1990s with the spread of less expensive desktop publishing systems. In the 2010s, inexpensive black and white flyers can be produced with just a personal computer, computer printer and photocopier. In the 2010s, the ordering of flyers through traditional printing services has been supplanted by Internet services. Customers send designs, review proofs online or via e-mail and receive the final products by mail (https://en.wikipedia.org/wiki/Flyer_(pamphlet)).

Flyers are not a new medium: prior to the War of American Independence some colonists were outraged with the Stamp Act (1765) and gathered together in anti-stamp act congresses and meetings. In these congresses they had to win support, and issued handbills and leaflets, pamphlets, along with other written paraphernalia, to do so (https://en.wikipedia.org/wiki/Flyer (pamphlet)).

In the 2000s, some jurisdictions have laws or ordinances banning or restricting leafleting or flyering in certain locations. Owners of private property may put up signs saying "Post No Bills"; this occurs particularly on wooden fences surrounding building sites or vacant lots (https://en.wikipedia.org/wiki/Flyer_(pamphlet)).

◊◊◊

Designing the Flyer

So, now that we know a little bit about the history of the pamphlet known as a flyer, I believe that it is safe to say that the flyer is perhaps the most commonly used; but absolutely misused and poorly designed communications vehicle on the entire MC Biker Set! I cannot believe some of the designs I see go out on flyers these days and I often wonder what people are thinking about when they design them. So, as the professional communicator of the MC you should be part and parcel to every flyer design that happens in your club and you should be hawkish in your stand against FLYER BS in FLYER DESIGN!

Now, I must admit that I have not seen your flyer but I probably do not have to. Since I was a graphic designer for about 10 years, published more than 10 magazines, designed more than 20 website/blogs, and have written for countless publications, as well as having published two books now (at the time of this publishing), I can say that I have evaluated tens of thousands of flyers for MCs and small businesses over the years and they all pretty much contain the same mistakes and missed opportunities. Also, studies have shown that flyers are only about 1% effective as advertising tools. For every 500 you put out you can expect only about 5 people to respond to them. That being the case, it is vital that you use this chapter to avoid common mistakes by creating flyers that will not generate you the business that you are looking to gain.

Here are some things to think about when designing your flyers:

1. Organize your flyer!
Put your ideas together. It's much easier to design an excellent flyer if you know everything you want to put on it in advance. Makes the design experience much more comfortable.

2. Put the most important thing your reader in your headline, not the most important thing to you!
A flyer is an advertisement not a business card. It needs to create a CALL TO ACTION! That call to action is for someone to spend some money to attend your event, buy your raffle, or whatever. Lots of folks use it like a business card and put their club information first. Many designers are also obsessed with creating the most outrageous cards that they miss the whole point of the flyer. For instance, I have seen so much booty on MC flyers that did not have fine girls at their party at all! Like, what was that? You have a girl sliding down a pole into some JELL-O® in front of a Hyabusa—but the address and cost of the event is in little-bitty letters so small you need a magnifying glass to see them! GIVE ME A BREAK! The funny thing is when you get to the party and there is not even one pole there to be danced on. So,...? What was the flyer trying to say about the party in the first place? Forgive me, I am lost!

Listen, your potential customers are not interested in how cool your card looks, your name; or even how big the booty is of the girl on the card! They are stingy. They care about themselves. They care about attending an event that will meet their own wants and needs. So, think a little bit about what will draw in visitors to attend your event, annual, ride or dance.

Instead of a girl on a pole dripping with JELL-O® and this caption: "Wildest Party in Atlanta You Need to Be There or Be Square!"
Maybe a picture of some dollar bills and a caption like this: *Win $500.00 for Your MC's General Fund while Enjoying the Best Party of the*

Year!"

Or;

"Win a Tricked out Harley at the Black Sabbath Annual Cash Prizes Given for Attendance!"

Or;

Black Sabbath Cash/Trophy Party/Annual Dance (Largest Male MC (8ft tall trophy)/Largest Female MC (8 ft. tall trophy)/Largest SC ($400)/Furthest Distance/ Cash Prizes + Trophies!

As you can see, when you are telling people the benefit of attending your party, dance, or function; you will get far more folks coming to hang out.

3. Think about what you are portraying as an MC before you put it on a flyer. You may drive people away!

One year, the Black Sabbath MC Atlanta Chapter thought it would be a magnificent idea to give a gun away at our annual. Well, what the hell? I mean were we not in the Dirty South? Down here in the South, people are gun nuts and crazy about their weapons. We put it on our annual flyer: (WIN A GUN!!! GLOCK 19) **Must be able to pass a background check to pick it up. ** We were amazed at the poor attendance at our annual. We lost money that year. Much later, after local clubs got to know us—like the next year when we were passing out flyers again, I had a lot of Presidents tell me, "Man I would have come to your annual last year, but with that 'gun' stuff all over you guy's flyers I just didn't know what kind of stuff we were going to be getting ourselves into coming to hang out with ya'll. Sure wish we knew what kind of cool cats you were then. We sure would have supported you!"

So, that gives you something to think about when you put a stripper on your flyer, but you want a lot of women from Social Clubs to come and join your event. You may not be putting out a message that they want to spend their money to see; especially if you are not going to have any strippers at the party. Then, does it make a whole lot of sense to put them on your flyer?

4. Solve problems with your flyers rather than just listing services!
Instead of listing tasks when asking people to help you with a community project, "Come help the Black Sabbath MC clean up the neighborhood." Consider making the flyer about asking your invitees to solve a problem. "Remove debris, hypodermic needles, and trash from the park so our children can play safely!" You can talk about yourself on the second line.... "With the Black Sabbath MC."

5. Do not close weakly! Close your card strongly! Try to get the money early!

- *Buy advanced tickets before (DATE), and receive $10 off.*
- *Buy 10 tickets or more before (DATE), and get a 15% off!*
- *Buy 10 tickets or more before (DATE) and everyone gets one free drink!*

You get the idea.

6. Do not forget the pass-along!
Never be too proud to beg. A great sentence to include is, "If you aren't coming pass this card to someone you know who will!" Granted most folks are going to throw the flyer away, but some can be moved by the 'call to action' to pass your flyer along!

7. Never leave the back side empty!!!
Do not be a cheapskate. Spend the extra money to go double-sided, high glossy flyers! A flyer with a blank, nice, juicy, white, empty back is nothing but an invitation to use to write a pretty girl's phone number on, write a grocery list on, or write directions to the doctor and the appointment date on. This means the flyer you spent money on to deliver your message is, instead, sitting in someone's wallet turned to the side of the phone number—never to display your message again until about a year or two after your event is long past-or worse your flag is turned over never to be seen again!

8. Resist the Junky Flyer!

Less is more in all graphic design. It is just the way it is. In today's marketing environment people are bombarded with way too much information all of the time. Consumers these days are only scanning information so you have a very small window to catch their attention. No matter what kind of marketing you are trying to accomplish, including flyer design, KEEP IT SIMPLE STUPID (K.I.S.S)! Less is more, and more is less. That simply means that the less time a person has to spend looking to get your message, the more of your message they will get. The more time they have to spend to get your message, the less of your message they will get because they will simply tune your message out!

9. Distribute more than once!

Studies show that most folks don't respond to a single advertisement. That is why the most famous hamburger joint in the world (with those golden arches) continues to run ads even though everyone knows who they are. So once you have done one flyer dusting. Do another one. Cover your area once or twice or three times over!

10. Did you know that you can test a flyer?

Flyers do not cost nearly as much as other advertising. If you are not sure about a headline or a particular flyer design compared to another. Print one, put it out, and then on the second dusting use the other one. Test the reaction. Then you will know which one to go with for your third dusting.

11. Double Up!

You can print create an ad on your flyer that is two-up; or two flyers on a single page. Cut the page in half and now you have two flyers for the price of one. Cool huh?

12. Proof READ!!!

Man, I hated when I printed ten thousand flyers and the address was off by one NUMBER!!! Money down the drain!

13. You can be broke and still advertise.
If on a budget, select a bright-colored or unique paper, and print with black ink. Use shades of gray to provide tones and contrasting on the background area.

14. Can you track your flyer?
Want to know how effective your flyers are? Create a way to track them! For instance, "Present this flyer at the door for a $5.00 discount!" Now you will know just how effective your flyer campaign was.

CHAPTER EIGHT
Website and Blog Management

The Design

If you want your MC's reputation, membership, and brand to grow; you will do well to have an engaging and powerful website. The MC's website will communicate the MC's message twenty-four hours per day seven days per week. It will be the go to area for general information about the MC for news, media, governmental agencies, and law enforcement. Indeed, gone are the days a successful MC can run without an interactive and professional website.

Though you may not be a web design expert, you will be responsible for managing and editing website content, and you may well be responsible for designing the website or putting together the specifications for a Web Master to design your MC's site. Why you? Well, because all public facing entities of the MC come under your domain as the professional communicator of the club. So cheer up. It is not so bad.

If you are called upon to build or design your MC's website, blog, or online newsletter; understand that there are many tools, services, and resources that are available to make it easier to design a professional looking website. However, if you know absolutely nothing about computers or website building you may want to hire a professional. While you focus on the content, you can leave the website design to the Web Master. If you are on a budget, you can choose a company like 1 And 1, and go with one of their template packages. Then, all you have to do is add pictures, stories, and links. The website design is as easy as putting things on a MS Word document! Presto! It will not be custom, but it can still look decent. In fact, www.blacksabbathmc.com was designed with a 1AND1 template in 2009. As of the writing of this book, it has served the BSMC Nation for the past seven years. Whatever you do do not get so caught up in web design that you do not get the website developed! You have a lot of responsibilities as PRO. Get the content put together, "supervise" a Web Master, and get on with other club business.

Here are some tips to get you moving quickly and on your way:

Step 1: Look at What Others Have Done
They say imitation is the greatest form of flattery so do not be ashamed to "borrow" design ideas from other MC's out there. Just peruse the sites of your favorite MC's and collect ideas for how you want your site to look. Then, you can convey those ideas to your Web Master or try your hand at doing it yourself. There are also plenty of books and online resources that will help you get started. If you are new and have not much experience do not try to reproduce extremely complicated or sophisticated sites as that can be a truly frustrating waste of efforts.

Step 2. Define Your Goals
Take the time to write out exactly what you are trying to accomplish with your site before you start building it. If you are working with a Web Master he/she will demand this. Do not try to just start designing pages without a design list. You can start with a statement list that describes what you want to do with your audience. For example:

The Black Sabbath MC Website should tell visitors:

- ○ Who we are, our name and logos
- ○ When we started
- ○ Our Mission Statement
- ○ History section will talk about our forefathers and club history
- ○ Locations of where all of our chapters and clubhouses are/addresses
- ○ Pictures and email addresses as well as contact information of all of our presidents
- ○ Club life section should talk about Black Sabbath leaders and trend setters
- ○ Membership section will deliver information about gaining membership
- ○ Charter & Rules section will deliver information for starting chapters in other areas
- ○ Sabbath Fallen section will graciously and respectfully list our dead and fallen
- ○ Sabbath Prospecting section will deliver information for prospecting as Black Sabbath
- ○ Magazine section will be our online magazine detailing Black Sabbath life in a Blog like format
- ○ History of Women in the MC will talk about BSMC SOTC and Goddesses
- ○ History of the Outlaw MC will talk about 99%er vs. 1%er MCs
- ○ RC vs. MC will deliver information about club variances
- ○ MC Club Basics will give newbies information about club life basis
- ○ Downloads will deliver BSMC downloadable: membership application/charter application/ other
- ○ Video/Pics section will deliver our galleries
- ○ Events section will list our events, dances, runs, and other

breaking information
- Find us is an interactive map that lists all of our locations nationwide
- Contact us lists contact information for BSMC VIPS, PROs, and others
- Guest Book is area for guest clubs to leave messages to be followed up by PRO
- Store delivers BSMC online store with E-Commerce plug that enables buying from the site
- Links to BSMC brother/sister clubs and social clubs websites
- BSMC Charitable Giving delivers information about all BSMC charities and pics/videos of BSMC's giving
- Social Media links deliver links to all BSMC social media sites
- News delivers breaking BSMC 'only' news
- Nomad Riders presents all BSMC Nomads
- From the National delivers secret messages to BSMC members only ***Secret Password Entry for members only***

Now you have a basic template from which to start. You can gather information and content to add to this format. For instance for the first bullet you might do something like this:

*Who we are, our name and logos: Welcome to the Site <**Headline**>*
*Welcome to the Black Sabbath M.C. website. We warmly invite you to surf these pages to discover who we are, what we are about, and why we have banded together to form a family of brothers and sisters. Dedicated to serving our country and communities, while creatively pursing the love, joy, and freedom of riding motorcycles; we welcome all riders, all styles, all bikes, all races, and both sexes! We are a breed apart! We've never done anything like the rest! <**Insert body**>*
*What We Do - A Brief History <**Headline**>*
The Black Sabbath Motorcycle Club is a LAW ABIDING, not-for-profit organization conceived in 1972 and established in 1974, on the South East side of San Diego California in the Mt. Hope neighborhood at 4280 Market Street. Our mission then wasn't very complicated, we were just group of seven African American men who rode our bikes mostly on Sundays and

*were similarly possessed with an insatiable appetite for custom building "Choppers" and race-bikes to impress the ladies and civilians, and to compete against all comers great and small. When our wives got tired of us meeting in our garages on Sundays and began complaining about us making noise in the neighborhoods; we realized it was time to form a motorcycle club and get ourselves a clubhouse. The Black Sabbath San Diego MC clubhouse is the longest standing clubhouse in San Diego - 40+ Years and STILL STRONG!! **<Body>***

*Our Colors **<Headline>***

*Our one-piece patch identifies us as a traditional, family-oriented, 99%er law abiding MC to other motorcycle club nations on biking sets around the world. Our colors are affectionately named "The Turtle Shell" because the huge 16 inch back patch resembles a turtle shell on the backs of most members. OUR COLORS DON'T RUN! Blood, sweat, and tears have been shed so that future generations of Black Sabbath could wear our colors with pride. The colors are honored as the symbol of the bond that binds the Mighty Black Sabbath MC Nation together. Our colors have been recognized on the biking set, starting in San Diego, California and extending from the shores of the Pacific Ocean, to the sands of the Atlantic Ocean, and all over the world since 1974. Blessed by the dominant Chosen Few MC Nation and the dominant Hells Angels MC Nation in San Diego, California as well as dominants in every city we have occupied since, we make no apologies for our colors. We boast proudly from within them. They have brought us no shame or disservice. We wear them with pride, never surrender them, never dip them, and never bring discredit upon them! **<body>***

Step 3. List the Features Your Site Will Need

Websites can have all kinds of features such as chat rooms, message boards, shopping carts, banner ads, and searchable databases. Here is some example of features that might go on the site listed above:

- Database program for mailing lists
- Shopping basket and secure server for taking online orders
- Traffic analysis software
- Access controls

- Private section and passwords for member's only section
- Email auto-responder for guests who leave comments

Step 4: Identify an Appropriate Website Host

The website host is the entity that has the servers and databases that display your website to the world. A poor hosting company can be your worst experience. I have always used 1AND1.com because they have sharp technical support that you can get to twenty-four hours per day. This allows you to get things fixed and handled early enough that you can get some sleep on a night! Not all hosts are alike. A cheaper option may mean no technical support or maybe not 24/7 technical support. You be the judge.

Step 5: Design the Site

Either use a pro, or do it yourself. I have always done my sites myself. Simply put, I always wanted to be a techie. If your MC has a budget you may hire someone. Let your available time and experience decide. As I mentioned before, you can go with a template design from your host company or you can use a content management software like WordPress to develop you site. WordPress is a great template website design program that gives you both a blog and a website simultaneously and there are zillions of free WordPress templates out there that you can utilize. Do some research to find out what is right for you.

◊◊◊

Gathering an Audience

It takes a lot of work to gather an audience to view your website. However, as the PRO it will be your responsibility to bring eyeballs to your website and social media sites to build the reputation of your MC and get their message to the MC's friends, supporters, and publics. Start by developing and working online relationships with other MCs. Make a checklist of every MC's site you can think of and every other type of site they may visit on the internet, then connect with each of those. There are a lot of ways to do this. For instance, you can write articles for motorcycle interest websites on safety or

MC life. At the end of the articles, leave the club name and URL. This brings eyeballs to your MC's site and sets your MC apart as a leader in trend-setting and thinking on those subject areas. You can post messages on other MC's visitor boards with your MC's URL left at the end of each post. It allows folks who have viewed that guest page to follow your link back to your MC's website. You can send out press releases, media alerts, and pitch letters about interesting subjects on your website; perhaps gaining an article or two in the local or area newspaper that will bring new eyes to your site. You can also trade links with other MC's and MC related sites. A link trade is: "I'll put your link on my site if you put my link on your site."

Search Engine Optimization (SEO)

I have to take a little time to talk about SEO as you may hear of it sooner or later. SEO has to do with your MC's placement on a website when someone does a search on a search engine like Google. If you have ever done a search, you know that most people do not look past the first page for what they are looking for. The idea of SEO is that if you are on that first page your site gets seen where others do not. And if you are at the top of that page then you get seen before anyone! Businesses try very hard to be at the top of a search engine page, so much so, that they will pay professional SEO specialists to develop their sites in a way that they will always appear at the top of search engines. SEO is as much an art as it is a science. It is something the new comer should steer clear of trying to master, and for Christ's sake do not DARE PAY anyone calling you on the phone to sell you this service. I do not care what they promise you. I am not going to go into great detail about all the specifications of executing great you SEO; there is just too much for me to attempt to cover the subject in this book as SEO is an entire book, or three, all by itself. I just want for you to know the term, and know that as soon as you start putting your site together you will get emails from so-called *SEO masters* who will promise you incredible results in placing your website at the top of every search engine in the world. It just is not that simple. Most of the folks selling those SEO services are scam artist (this has been my experience) so make your site full of worthy content, and do some of the other things I mentioned above. Over time, your site will be bristling with visitors.

◊◊◊

Keep the Site Updated

Keeping a website up-to-date is a royal pain in the rear end, but like most things a PRO does, it is a must. People will not return to your site if your info is not fresh and ever changing. With all of the other responsibilities you have, updating a site every day may simply be out of the question. You can enlist someone to make the physical updates while your provide the content or get members to help out (always hard to do). Some of the nagging things to remember that your members will notice before you do:

- Changes in positions and titles of officers and members
- Removing people that are no longer in the club
- Including recognition of members who have done something of note in the MC
- Changes of email addresses or phone numbers
- Changes in the physical addresses of new clubhouses
- Addition of pictures members have of events they have attended

CHAPTER NINE
Social Media

Social Media Operations

Merriam-Webster defines social media as, "Forms of electronic communication (as Web sites for social networking and microblogging) through which users create online communities to share information, ideas, personal messages, and other content (as videos)."

Social media currently dominates the Internet in terms of the tool that is most used by folks to send and receive information to their networks. If your MC has social media sites, they are probably viewed far more than your website; and for good reason. Social media sites are easy to update. Have fresh new information on them. The latest pictures can get uploaded from a smart phone or tablet. Still, there is an element of control that you do not have on your social media sites because, after all, they do not belong to you. If your MC magically or unknowingly violates a social media site's terms of service, its presence can be deleted and there will be nothing that anyone can do about it. So, keep your website as the "official" information dissemination spot for your MC's internet presence and use social media sites to compliment your website.

There are several social media sites to which your MC could

belong. I say, the more the merrier. There are management programs and apps that you can download that will allow you to make a change on one social media site and it will update the rest of them simultaneously. There just is not enough space in this book to talk a lot about all of the types of social media sites there are. The important thing is not to let them get out of hand. If it gets too unruly just delete some and start over again with it later if you want. Always enlist help from someone in the MC.

◊◊◊

Social Media Policy for MCs

Every MC should have a social media policy to govern how its members access and use social media and personal blogs. If you are recruiting young people into your MC you must understand that they use all of the various kinds of chats, pages, group apps, and everything else you can imagine. I do not list the names because in five or ten years the ones that I list now will not even be relevant then. So, what is a PRO to do? It is ironic but the laws of the MC never change, yet folks get on social media and show/tell the world every single thing going on in their lives INCLUDING the MC's business; which is certainly against protocol.

My rule of thumb is that whenever a member creates a page in the name of our MC that the PRO, the President and the Sgt at Arms have ADMIN rights to that page. Meaning, we can go in and delete anything we want without having to ask any questions about it. This is important because an idiot on the Book can ruin the entire image of the MC, start a club war, or get some innocent person in the MC hurt at a gas pump, knowing nothing about what that idiot ever even typed in the first place! As you are the guardian of the MC's reputation you must be on the ball in training, education, and monitoring your folks' social media blog entries.

You also have to beware of what I call "Cyber-Banging" which is like gang banging only from behind a computer screen. Club cyber-bangers are dangerous to the reputation of the MC. Their antics and bullying can start club wars and cause members to get hurt. You can have a member say something about a club in Atlanta and one of your innocent members in Houston get his head knocked off at a gas station by someone from an MC he's never heard of or wronged. The lesson club members must learn is that there is no I in MC. If you say or do something negative it can have bad repressions for the entire MC.

Another problem to look for, is fighting between club members. I cannot tell you the number of folks who find it necessary to run the MC's business on social media as they say good bye or go to hell. Make sure that your policies and bylaws are amended to include punishments for such actions—including sanctions against you if you leave the MC with that kind of an exit.

For instance, I once had a guy make a racist statement against a dominant MC on the Book after that MC was featured in the news for a violent act. He said that they were worthless such and such(es) and they could kiss his a**. He used a racial epithet and said he had better not ever see one or he would give him a piece or two of his mind! The crazy thing about it was that his user name was his riding name that ended with Black Sabbath (killerjoeblacksabbath)! When I called him he was completely oblivious to the nonsense in which he was partaking. I asked him, "Hey man. You do know that kind of nonsensible rhetoric gets people killed right? And, probably the person killed won't be you. It will be one of your innocent brothers somewhere just minding his own business."

The best idea is to write some kind of Internet and Social Media Policy to which club members will have to adhere so that when they do this kind of thing, you can fire them and move on to other business:

Sample MC Internet/Social Media Blogging Policy

In general, the Black Sabbath MC views personal websites, weblogs, and social media portals positively; and it respects the right of members to use them as a medium of self-expression. If you choose to identify yourself as a Black Sabbath MC member or to discuss matters related to our MC on your website or weblog, please bear in mind, that although you and we view your website, weblog, or social media portal as a personal project and a medium of personal expression; some readers may, nonetheless view you as a de facto spokesperson for the Mighty Black Sabbath Motorcycle Club Nation. In light of this possibility, we insist that you observe the following guidelines:

1. Please make it clear to your readers that the views you express are yours alone and that they do not necessarily reflect the views of the Black Sabbath MC Nation. To help reduce the potential for confusion, put the following notice – or something similar – in a reasonably prominent place on your site (e.g., at the bottom of your "about me" page).

2. The views expressed on this website/weblog/page are mine alone and do not necessarily reflect the views of the Mighty Black Sabbath MC Nation.

3. Avoid disclosing any information that is MC Business! If you have to ask yourself, "I wonder if that is MC Business?" the answer is that it probably is and you shouldn't be talking about it!

4. Do not infringe on MC intellectual properties, deface, or otherwise cause harm or damage the Mighty Black Sabbath MC Nation's reputation. To avoid conflicts or discrepancies consult the PRO, VP, or President if you have questions about the appropriateness of publishing information related to the MC's business on your sites or pages.

5. Since your site or blog is a public space, be as respectful to the MC, our members, our publics, our brother/sister clubs and affiliates, and others (including our enemies) as the MC itself endeavors to be.

6. You may provide a link from your sites to our website. However you will require permission to use Black Sabbath MC Nation trademarks or reproduce MC materials on your sites.

7. Understand that the Mighty Black Sabbath MC Nation may request that you temporarily confine your website, social media, or weblog commentary to topics unrelated to the MC community (or, in rare cases, that you temporarily or permanently suspend your website, social media, or weblog activity altogether) if it

believes this is necessary or advisable to ensure safety of our members, avoid club wars, or other dangerous situations.

8. *Some subjects can invite an MC to MC war! Be careful discussing things where emotions run high (e.g. politics, religion, who is doing who) and show respect for others' opinions.*

9. *If you #!%#@# up! Correct it immediately and be clear about what you've done to fix it. Contact the PRO if it's really bad!*

10. *Don't even think about it…. Talking about 1%er MC business, incidents that happen on the MC Set, negative thoughts about club members, officers or policies, speculating about rumors, legal issues of other MCs, future club activities, giving out personal information about members or officers, posting confidential or non-public information, or responding to an offensive or negative post by anyone! There's no winner in that game so don't be the one to get the shit started!*

11. *Members should verify ANY KIND OF RUMOR with credible sources before posting or tweeting about it.*

If you have any questions about these guidelines or any matter related to your site that these guidelines do not address, please direct them to the PRO, VP, or Prez.

Limiting Official Fan Page and Official MC Accounts

You may want to give thought to making policies and bylaws that constrain the launching of official fan pages and other social media accounts to just the PRO or a few select individuals. Fan pages and other Social Media accounts can be made by any member at any time and they are very easy to lose control of, so constraining who can make them stops the problem before it begins.

Beware Who Has Admin Rights

You have to really think through who has admin rights to official MC fan pages, websites, and other online properties. In one instance, a rogue member that had admin rights kicked all of the other administrators off of the site and took over the site for a few months. The member then attempted to do everything possible to ruin the reputation of the MC by posting the craziest and most damaging things to the MC he could think to post. It was very difficult to get that page back because we were absolutely unable to get through to Facebook to get the page taken down. Keep this in mind when you are assigning admin rights.

CHAPTER TEN
Professional Photography

Photo Shoots

It has been said that a picture is worth a thousand words. If that is the case (and believe me it is), then nothing is the PRO's best friend more than an excellent photographer and the best pictures he/she can create. You will find that pictures will be invaluable for PR purposes. You can send pictures with media kits and press releases and gain a lot of traction for PR purposes. News agencies love great pictures to put in their papers and great videos to use in their video clips. You can also document the MC's history for posterity with great pictures from professional photo shoots. For that reason I thought I would take the rest of this chapter to give you a crash course on photo shoots.

Yes, you can use the pictures taken on your cell phone to take excellent pictures, and of course, you can gather around Picture Man Wynne at the Round Up; those are excellent pictures too! However, if you want your pictures to tell a story and convey targeted ideas, consider using a professional photographer with lights, helpers, and diffusion shades to see what kind of magic a professional photo shoot can deliver.

When it comes to managing any type of shoot, you need two things: organization and a strategy. As the size of the shoot increases, so does the complexity of its logistics and the details you and your team are responsible for managing. Hiring the right crew – and enough crew – will be a key part of a successful strategy and well-executed shoot.

Crash Course in Managing a Photo shoot

- Plan as many details as possible from the MC before you get started. Are you using models for some kind of sexy bike shoot or are you documenting how many folks the MC has? Maybe you are shooting a music video the MC is making, a documentary, or shooting some pictures of the MC helping the needy. You will need to create a production list, which is the written plan for the photographs you want to capture to consider your shoot a success.
- Realize that you are the PRO and you might not know everything you need to know about the photo shoot so do not try to be an expert where you are not. Get a qualified professional photographer who complements your style and bring any skills you lack to the table. All great photographers surround themselves with crew members who enhance their strengths and take personal responsibility for their actions—so once you identify one trust him to do his job.
  - You can determine if your photographer is good (or not) by looking at his portfolio (an album or group of albums that display the photographer's work) and by checking with his list of references to see what others he has worked for have to say about him. If he is shooting motorcycles, it will be a plus if he has shot them before. For instance, most folks who shoot models for motorcycle magazines also realize that readers want to see as much of the motorcycle as they do the model posing on it. That is just the crazy thing about bikers and motorcycles.

So, a good motorcycle photographer will show you a portfolio that you will be able to see a demonstrated ability to bring to full view the bike and the model at the same time. Believe me, it took a couple of years for me to get that technique together.

- On the day of the shoot be sure to have layouts and your shot list ready, on set, so you can keep track of the details as you go along. Layouts or visual guidelines that will help your photographer accurately shoot your project. If they do not have specific comps for the shoot, you can give the photographer tear sheets from other magazines or sketches to help him/her to see the vision you have in your mind. Be sure anything and everything you are asking for from the photographer is exactly what you estimate in the budget. Make sure he is on board for the hours you need him to work, for the price, and for what will be considered a successful shoot. For example, a photographer may tell you he only shoots for a max of four hours for a certain price—yet, after you get to the location several delays may occur with makeup, the weather, or whatever. Make sure that he does not come up to you four hours later—after you have only been shooting for thirty minutes, with his hand out demanding more money. It is better to have photographers bid by the photo shoot and not the hour when you are first getting started in the game.

- Location, location, location. Go out with your photographer and pre-scout your locations. Make sure you can get the subjects and their bikes there in the time budget and that you have permission or have paid to be there. For instance there are many places that you will have to pay to shoot at or that may not allow any shooting at all. If you really want to shoot there but you do not want to pay or you do not have permission, you have hit fast, move fast, get your shots, and get the hell out of there! You want to be positive you have the correct location, the correct number of bikes in the shots, and that the props or models in place that you want to use.

- There are best times to shoot outdoors because sunlight means EVERYTHING. Consider this though, the sunlight is the same color and temperature twice per day; in the morning and in the evening. So, the beautiful sun you get when the sun is coming up is the same beautiful sun you get when the sun is going down. I always like to shoot at first light. There is a reason for this. If my production crew is running late or there are any delays—even if I miss the beautiful sun and I am now shooting towards noon (which is the absolute worst time to shoot African American people in that harsh light), I can STILL get my photo shoot done because I have all day. Shooting in the evening means that if you are late and you miss the light you will have to shoot tomorrow. This incurs more costs!

- Since the advent of digital photography today's photographers get shot happy and want to shoot ten thousand pictures because you can shoot almost an unlimited amount of shots on any photo shoot. I come from the days when you had to pay for every roll of film, then pay to develop that roll also. Thus, it was eight dollars to buy the roll and twelve dollars to develop it. So, we got the shoot done with as few rolls as humanly possible to get the job handled! I can tell you from personal experience that NO ONE needs two thousand photographs from a single photo shoot! Get some idea of how many shots you actually think you are going to use, get the photographer on the business, and then get the hell out of there!

- Consider wardrobe and makeup. Yes, dudes need makeup too if you want those excellent shots. A wardrobe stylist can assist you in making sure that everyone looks uniform, has the right patches on, etc. The wardrobe stylist could be a sharp Prospect. It does not have to cost a lot of money.

- Consider having communications devices like walkie-talkies. They are invaluable when you have models dressing up the hill and your photo shoot is down the hill.

- A clear production schedule allows the entire crew to know what is happening during pre-production, on the actual shoot day(s), and during post-production.
- Consider having security at your shoot. If you are shooting models you can keep passer byers doing just that; passing by.
- Keep the set professional. If you have models in bathing suits on bikes, keep the MC Full Patch brothers from jeering at the women. It is a good way to catch a sexual harassment lawsuit!
- Professional photographers are tried-and-true experts. They understand how to achieve your goals in photography, and they will work quickly often serving as the on-the-spot creative director too. Do not be afraid to hold these photographers to a higher standard, and be certain that you review their portfolios. For a professional photographer in 2016, you might expect to pay five hundred dollars to five thousand dollars for a day of shooting.
- You will need a release from the photographer that includes perpetual, worldwide rights for you to use their photographs. That is right, even though he is shooting your people and your colors and your members and your models—he still owns his work. You will not own it until he releases it to you through a photographer's release. In my releases, I only allow the photographer the right to use the photographs in his portfolio ONLY. If he cannot agree to that, and to sign all of the rights over to me—there is no agreement.
- You will need a model release from your members and models who are featured on the shoot that includes perpetual, worldwide rights for you to use their images for the MC's marketing and promotional purposes. You can get examples of model releases and photographer releases free from many places on the Internet. Just do a search for

model release or photographer release.

- Always hire the models. Friends and family members might seem like an easy and obvious choice for models, and there are certainly many PROs who take this approach. But friends and family members are rarely experienced. They are less likely to know how to pose or take direction, and using them can slow down a photo shoot. That being said, you can get free models and photographers from web sites like www.modelmayhem.com. These kinds of websites were designed to give up and coming photographers, makeup artists, and models a place to collaborate and get together to exchange goods and services. They place their portfolios online and they seek each other out to trade time for photographs (TFP) or time for a CD (TFCD) or both (TFP/CD). That means we shoot for free and we all benefit from the pictures that are created. Then, we can use these pictures in our portfolios to get paid work. You can get the free models and photographers because many want to do bike shoots and your MC might have the mighty fine bikes they want to shoot on! It is something you may offer for their portfolios. You can find some awesome young photographers and models on sites like these. Although, you can also find some very inexperienced people, who flake out, no show/no call, or need more direction than you may be qualified to provide. Remember, you often get what you pay for in these situations. However, since I've been a photographer for decades, I have had incredible success utilizing these kinds of sites. If you are hiring models in 2016, you could pay one hundred dollars to fifteen hundred dollars per day for professional models.
- Be careful of the photographer who continually says, "I'll fix that in the editing" on the set. No amount of editing in Adobe Photoshop will suffice for proper capturing of the subject when shooting on the set. You cannot add light in the picture where no light existed when the picture was taken and so forth. If you hear the photographer saying that time and time again, pull him to the side and remind him

that you will not be paying for B.S.!

- There will be boxes to carry, photographic reflectors and diffusers to hold, and models to be tended. These are the jobs belonging to your crew. The crew can be the MC. Again, keep them professional. If someone cannot knock off the cat calls, dismiss him and put him up on charges with the President. Grown folks have little time to play with kids.

- Photographers can be lazy and procrastinators when it comes to getting your pictures back to you! Do not pay them until you have everything they are supposed to deliver. If they are supposed to do airbrushing and other techniques make sure you have ALL OF THAT BEFORE you pay. After your money is spent it sometimes becomes nearly impossible to find those guys!

- Having a laptop or monitor on set will allow you to preview pictures so you can determine how well the shoot is going and make adjustments if necessary.

- Bring extra printed copies of your lists to the shoot. This will help your team (and you!) stay on schedule. This will also allow your crew and models to be proactive, and plan ahead for upcoming scenes.

- Clean up along the way. It is much easier to stay organized and less overwhelming at the end if you clean up along the way.

- Rent equipment from a reputable place.

- If you want to keep people on the set for long periods of time consider a bucket of chicken, some fruit, and lots of water or soda. Plan ahead to have somewhere folks can relieve themselves (restroom) as well.

- Remind your models of shoot expectations a day or so before the shoot. A friendly reminder will go a long way. Send them the site schedule. Remind your models about the importance of being on time and being flexible with their time. Remind them of any props or wardrobe they are expected to wear or bring. And do not forget to give them the address of the shoot and contact information of someone on set to get in touch with if something comes up.

- Make the models feel comfortable. This is especially important if you did not hire professional models. Chat with the models and provide strong art direction so that they feel comfortable and understand the expectations. Most of all have fun! It will shine through in the images.

Okay, that was your crash course in running a photo shoot. A video shoot works much the same way only everything is moving. You will need to have a director, if it is not you. I am sure you get the point.

CHAPTER ELEVEN
Injuries/Hospitalizations/Death

Interview with a National PRO

Monica "Poochie" Peete

In writing this book I had the pleasure to reach out to some incredibly knowledgeable PROs on the MC Biker Set. One in particular was Monica 'Poochie' Peete. Peete is the National PRO for the FrontRunnerz MC. FrontRunnerz is a fast growing MC that started in Atlanta about 12 years ago. I called her up to ask her what she thought about The MC PRO's Bible's concept and delivery.

John: "Hey Poochie, I'm nearly finished writing the PRO's Bible, and I wanted to know if there might be anything I should add that could help my readers?

Poochie: "Did you talk about how PROs should handle hospitalizations of members, injuries, and death announcements?"

John: "Aaaahhh, heck Poochie man I never even THOUGHT about that! Poochie, I love you 'cause you always be on your sh**!"

Poochie: "That's my job John. I'm a National PRO. I got to be on it"

John: "Please tell the folks how to do that part of the job then, the floor is all yours. It's time for your 15 minutes of fame because you are now published!"

From Poochie National PRO of the FrontRunnerz MC

There are several factors a PRO must take into consideration when dealing with the intricacies of illnesses, wrecks, accidents, and death among the members of the MC. Many of the situations will produce competing challenges the PRO must navigate that will affect successful outcomes for the MC and the member's family. Here are some scenarios I have faced:

Illnesses:

Illnesses can be incredibly tragic events in the lives of members and their families. When a member gets a diagnosis of liver or kidney failure, advanced staged cancer, AIDS, heart dementia, or some other debilitating illness; they are faced with a life crisis that they may not be equipped to handle. Because the nature of MCs is for members to be nearly completely involved in all aspects of one another's lives, there can be a lot of pressure placed on a member that will not be good for them. The resulting stress can have negative consequences on the member's health, state of mind, and wellbeing; and could cause them to deteriorate more quickly than they would have. So, the PRO must be especially alert and forward thinking in these matters.

There is no cookie cutter process to follow when handling these events. So, the PRO must be wise. Because of the nature of the PRO's business, the PRO often has to build relationships throughout the MC community. The MC community members tend to approach the PRO, because the PRO is known to be someone they can establish trust in. Members will bring things to the PRO that they would never tell anyone else, or may use the PRO as a sounding board to determine who and what they should tell about their situation. A PRO cannot be messy! The PRO must know when to be silent, when to listen, and when to give advice. The PRO duty may be to the guard the reputation of the MC or in some cases to guard the privacy and dignity of the member. Balancing the competing interests of the MC wanting to know as much as they can about their extended family member, the member's need for dignity and privacy, and the family's natural need to encircle the member and protect them from the outside (and in many cases the MC will always be considered outsiders), can be a daunting task that can also put tremendous stress and pressure on the PRO.

Members handle the challenges of facing life's obstacles differently. You may have a member tell you, "I'm going in for a cancer operation. I'm not going to tell anyone but you so if something happens to me and I don't' make it then you can tell everyone what happened to me, and that I loved them all."

Now, you are sharing this awful burden with the member, and it can be taxing. So, time progresses, and the member is not seen very often, misses some meetings, perhaps an assignment or two; what happens when other members start questioning this member's character- when the member stops showing up for rides and events as often? The PRO knows the member is sick and going through chemo after the surgery but none of the members know and the PRO has sworn you to silence. What do you say when rumors start to run rampant and members start calling for the sick member's colors or to be fined, suspended, or kicked out of the club? How skillfully will you manage the situation to protect the member's reputation while guarding her privacy? In such cases it's often the reputation and trustworthiness of the PRO, themselves, that can save the day.

For instance, if you told the President, "There are some issues that I've been made aware of with member X, that I cannot share about her at this time, but I can assure you that her inability to show up for functions is through no fault of her own and cannot be helped. The member will likely return in a few months, so chill everyone out and take the heat for her sir."

If your word as PRO is impeccable the President could trust you enough take the proper steps on your word alone. A PRO survives on their ability at relationship building. A PRO works hard day and night to be a credible source to which people can turn and know their information will be appropriately handled. A PRO does not spill, unnecessarily, information just to be running off at the mouth. If a PRO is in a club and an intoxicated member of another MC starts running his mouth negatively about his club does a PRO run and tell that MC's President? Or does the PRO realize the member is drunk and running off at the mouth and keep?

The Pro is a professional communicator. The PRO must think wisely when handling situations that involve member illnesses. The PRO has to be good about stopping rumors in their tracks. Rumors help no one, especially since most of them are not based in facts. To take the above scenario to another level let us consider that perhaps someone in the MC heard from a nurse friend of theirs, who works on the cancer ward, that there was a member of your MC recovering from an operation on her ward. The nurse starts spreading rumors that purportedly convey that the member's illness is even worse than it actually is. The member knows you are the only one she told in the MC so this rumor floating around the club could have negative repercussions on your reputation as the suffering member may potentially blame you for the rumor. The ironic thing about rumors is that it is nearly impossible to even tell where they start most times, but folks seem believe them no matter what. Now that the rumors are spreading something must be done to respect your member's wishes. It would be incumbent upon you to get to the President and shut the rumor mill down, educating the offending members that spreading rumors about the private medical details of a another member, especially without permission to do so—is not appropriate, nor will it be tolerated. Maybe even a club meeting to get this information out may be in order. Being quick to respond to member needs is an important quality.

Missing Persons

Because of relationships I have built across the Set with multiple MCs over the years, I often feel like I am not just my MC's PRO but kind of all MC's PRO in general. I find it amazing that people will call me from another part of the country to ask for information about a function in Mississippi. "Heck I'm not even in Mississippi." I might say.

"But we know you know everything that's going on so tell us about that function in Mississippi," they might reply.

I have also found this to be the case in missing person's reports. It is difficult to find out a motorcyclist has died doing something they love, yet family is unable to be immediately contacted because of the lack of identification on the motorcyclist at the time of death. A witness may have seen the accident but does not have information to contact the motorcyclist's family. Folks worked diligently to try to put two and two together and the motorcycle community set lights up trying to identify the person. A timer starts ticking as the man's body lies in the hospital unclaimed. The ticking clock is vital because many hospitals will cremate an unclaimed body after so many days; so it was important to find out what hospital this person was in, get the motorcyclist identified and to their family. As PROs, you have to band together to find out who the person was and claimed, so the family can prepare for the proper burial.

Again, one of the biggest things you have to combat is the rampant rumors. It is crazy what people will pick up the phone and say, or things people will type on social media without even considering the consequences. Misidentification is another problem that can have serious emotional consequences on family members:

- Never put anything out that you have not confirmed; especially on social media
- Do not repeat gossip
- Do not release information before getting permission from the family
- Work quickly among hospitals, law enforcement, and other agencies to find missing

Family Considerations:

Working with families can be touchy. Unless you are dealing with a family that has been involved with the Set for generations, most will never understand the bond a brother or a sister has with their MC. They will almost never see the importance of the MC as an extended family, and many will be jealous because lots of members spend more time with the MC than with their blood families. So, when you are dealing with a family of ill, missing or member that has passed; please try to be very professional and cautious so as not to become wrapped up in under currents, family feuds, or disagreements between the MC and the family. Remember these things:

- The family is blood the MC will never be. The family has all legal rights so their wishes must be obeyed.
- It is not the PROs responsibility to plan funerals, etc. Let the family do that. You are there to assist them in any way they want to accept.

- Before you release any information confirm it with the family first!

> - The family may not want details of a person's injuries released to the public.
> - The family may not want details of a person's injuries floating around on social media.
> - The family may want to hold information until distant relatives have been informed.
> - The family may not want the MC involved in any way.
> - The family may be hostile towards the MC community because the family may had never wanted the member to own a motorcycle in the first place. They may feel like they were right all along about the danger of motorcycle riding, and the MC was that group that empowered their family member to die.

As you can see working with the family to achieve their wishes during times of crisis or death can be a tough proposition. Stay professional, stay focused, and stay committed.

Deaths:

Handling the death or passing of a member is never routine. If the person died in a motorcycle wreck, you could be dealing with an irate family. If the person died of an illness it may be a different situation. But what if a person dies of violence i.e. maybe they got shot by another member of your MC? Now you have to deal with an angry family that cannot see the passion of an MC whose member's kill one another. You can see how it can all be twisted. Imagine if a member gets killed by a member of an outlaw MC? Now, you have the complexities of handling information and people, while trying to keep rumors down and tempers that could spark a club shooting war. Sound judgment and wise decision making is the key:

- Positive identification is necessary before speculating
- Do not release information without the family's permission (wait, I already said that... Hmmmm)
- Work within the MC's policy and the family's wishes to send flowers etc.
- Some family's may want a 'Go Fund Me' account setup where others may want something else; be prepared
- Help the President prepare his speech for the funeral
- Check with the family to see if they want a club escort or MC pallbearers
- Check with the President on the MCs policies for handling the colors of the dead
- Handle the press with press conferences, press releases, etc.

CHAPTER TWELEVE
Where to From Here

The Progression from PRO

Monica "Poochie" Peete

Once you have worked as a PRO for some time and mastered the skills of the PRO, you will look around to decide where your next MC opportunity will be. You may consider being a Sgt-at-Arms, Business Manager, or something else. However, it has been my observation that more and more PROs are going from PRO directly to the Presidency of an MC. Once you have spent time fighting for the MC, defending its reputation, and managing its publics; you will find that few are better at putting out the MC's message or selling the merits of the MC than yourself. I can think of at least seven PROs that I have known who recently went directly to President after their PRO terms ended. A PRO winds up working everyday with all departments within the MC and with MCs on the Set across many state lines. After the successful career of a PRO, you will have a Rolodex full of movers and shakers numbers throughout the MC community. A PRO is able to pick up the phone and make things happen. Notice that a PRO will build relationships with charities, government officials, the press, law enforcement, and business leaders. National Presidents, VPs, Presidents, and VIP will become accessible to easily you, providing vast knowledge and information in a quick manner. As a new leader, the PRO will be well tested and honed, because your expertise is invaluable to the MC. Many people will think that they can be a PRO, but so many are wrong. It is not what they think it is. The PRO demonstrated is more than just the party person, but a force to be reckoned. Find your new direction, open your wings, and fly!

CHAPTER THIRTEEN
Club to Club Relations

MC to MC

MC to MC relationships have long been the responsibility of the Secretary in traditional MCs. If it is to be that an MC will open the position of PRO, then it would seem natural that MC to MC relations will switch to the PRO as he/she is better equipped to handle this position. As the totality of this book has demonstrated, a PRO will possess the communication, networking, media management, and reputation management skills that are not mandated for a traditional secretary to master in any book on MC protocol or descriptions of that club job. It will therefore be up to the PRO to forge relationships between MCs, shore up the reputation, and build the stature of the MC; while ensuring that the MC has allies and brother/sister clubs at its disposal to support its events, runs, and best interests.

Of significant importance to today's MCs, is the number of quality MC to MC relationships it can foster—if it wants to be a successful contender on the MC Biker Set. When MC Secretaries were responsible for cultivating these relationships, before email, instant messages, and social media chats rooms; club Secretaries would trade mail and post cards between the MC and brother/sister clubs. During church, the Secretary would read the letters, bulletins, invitations, and cards to the members. Clubs would invite each other to participate in events, runs, parties, and cookouts. When the MC threw an event there were always going to be a certain number of allied clubs that the MC knew would be there. These clubs comprised a base of support for the MC. You always knew who your friends were. You could always tell who your friends were. Your allied clubs showed up for your funerals, lent their trailers when your scoot broke down, and you would always see a whole bunch of their cuts where ever your cuts were.

The PRO will have to master the skills of MC to MC communications once exercised by the MC's Secretary. You will be a master at networking. You will have your ear to the ground to spot trends, rumors, and swells. You will use your intuition to advise your President of when your brother and sister clubs need the MC's participation. When it comes to brother and sister clubs, you will know when their members are sick, who needs a card, who needs a visit in the hospital, who is having a birthday, and where folks will be throwing a get together on fight night. This information you will convey to the MC. For instance, a couple of years ago, two brothers in an allied club were run over on a highway from behind by a car at a construction site. Our PRO heard of the accident on the wires and the BSMC was at the hospital, visiting, providing, support and food for the family until those brother's MC got there. To this day, years later, that MC can be found at any event we throw. In another time, when a club founder died, the BSMC nation rode to the funeral with scores of motorcycles to show our allegiance. The PRO provided us with all of the information and coordinated with the local chapter President to ensure we were all there at the appointed place and time.

As PRO, you will master the art of organizational communications. You are a people person and people are your field of expertise. You will develop many relationships beyond your own club members and you will be sought after to deliver communications between other MCs and your MC. You need to be simply a conduit of information. You are the pipe through which the information flows. You do not color the information or feed it through your filters. You do not attach to politics, nor do you involve yourself in matters between Presidents, wars, or disagreements. It is not your job to solve those kinds of problems. You are not a club negotiator. That is the President's job. Learn to understand when it is time to pass the issue on and remove yourself from it. You are a communicator not a commander. It is not your job to interpret intention—you simply deliver the message. You may deliver inflection but never intention. Do not be messy. Stay above the fray.

◇◇◇

Progression of the PRO

So, yes. I learn about most of the parties, runs, charity drives, protests, and almost everything else I go to from the various chapter PROs in the Mighty Black Sabbath MC Nation. Yes, there are many of my chapters who have PROs and some who do not. In our case, NOT the mother chapter, of course, they are still hard core old school so they have a Secretary. I am not really sure when or where the PRO position hit our MC. I would just hear from folks through email or something, who would sign off of the email with "PRO"—and honestly for a couple of years I probably did not even know what the hell they were talking about. I would look on my GroupMe or What'sApp and there would be a list of flyers of stuff to do and meet up times on the phone—from the PRO. I thought, "Hmm that's convenient." I think I finally said one day, "Oh PRO… Public Relations Officer… I get it! We got those in the club now!? Nobody told me, hell I'm the National I need to pick my game up!"

That is probably about the time I started to hear all of the traditional MCs and 1%ers railing against the idea of the PRO and decrying what a waste the job was. Still, I have been around for a minute and I have always noticed that when folks start bellyaching about change—mostly it is because that change is real and that change brings about positive results. So, as I began looking at what our so called PROs thought they were doing. I sat down and got out of their way. I have watched them develop their craft, within the MC, over the past seven years. Then, as a worthy leader I set out to define what their role would be within our nation, and I thought this work might help other MC's PROs so voilà! Another book. I will share with you that most of my books are actually conceived from writings I author for my own MC.

CHAPTER FOURTEEN
Annual Dances and Parties

The Annual Dance

This is probably my smallest chapter, and is ironically, what the PRO is most known for doing.

Still, I promise to be brief here. This is the chapter where I talk about planning club parties, annual dances, attending dances and passing out flyers. "What is a PRO except a glorified flyer dispenser?" someone once sarcastically stated.

Well, if you've been reading this book you have learned that dispensing flyers is probably one of the lowest priority tasks that are on your agenda and as such, takes up the least amount of your time. Your answer to a question like that could be, "I design the flyers and make sure the information on them is correct. The MC dispenses them."

We have to talk about planning the annual dance as it is one of the biggest events, for most MCs, of the year. I do not plan a lot of annual dances, the MC does that, and I think that is probably the biggest lesson for the PRO. It's your job to market, inform, and disseminate information to further the MC's agenda, best interests, guard its reputation and manage its publics. If you are good at that, you will find the MC wanting to throw you on a bunch of projects (like party planning committee) which you can accept, but is really not a part of your PRO job! So, let them plan the parties, runs, dances, etc., and then you work with them to get the messages OUT! Let them pick the venues, times, and dates; then you design the flyers for THEM to pass out! Of course, you will pass some out too and probably hark the dances better than anyone else, but let the MC work on its own behalf while you help them by guiding the communications.

For instance, when I was a President of the Atlanta chapter, I got many calls from Presidents to ask me, personally, if I would support their events. This is a handshaking protocol that goes on between Presidents. The President would assure me that he would return the favor when it was time for my chapter to throw its event. This was a commitment the President could naturally make of his chapter. Presidents handshaking with Presidents is a long held tradition in the MC world. However, when I started getting calls from PROs I would instantly feel somewhat insulted. Why would a non-decision maker assume that he/she should call a President to represent a club, other than to tell me, "Hold on a second, I'm calling you for my Prez, let me put him on the phone."

Stay in your lane. It is more appropriate for you to put together a list of Presidents for the Prez to call and then sit there and dial each number for him, if you have to, and pass the phone to him, than it is for you to call Presidents and make club commitments with an authority your position does not have. To call a President and tell him that your Prez said, "We'll support you if you support us" makes your President seem lazy or seem like he is too important or busy to call my insignificant club. Hell no, we ain't coming!

◊◊◊

Interview with S.A.T.

Case Study

Interview with Terri "S.A.T." Benn former PRO for the Atlanta Chapter about club annuals:

Terri S.A.T. Benn

Black Dragon: *"S.A.T. what would you describe as the duties of the PRO?"*

S.A.T.: *"Well, Dragon the PRO is a relationship builder. She should pride herself in developing RELATIONSHIPS! Actually, it may be easier to say what the PRO is not."*

Black Dragon: *"Well, what is not the Pro then?"*

S.A.T. *"Okay, the PRO is not the Flyer-passer-outer. The PRO is not the 'ho' of the club. The PRO is not be the 'party-all-nighter' person. The PRO wants to see all MCs grow and develop. And in so doing, she wants to figure out how she can aid in the growth and development of all MCs. For instance, a good PRO doesn't attend parties with the sole purpose of getting other MCs to attend her MC's party. Instead she goes because she has a GENUINE interest in supporting other MCs and seeing them do well. In so doing she BUILDS RELATIONSHIPS that, after a while, eventually, develop into families."*

Black Dragon: *"So, how do you go about building these relationships?"*

S.A.T.: *"Well now, this is weird now-a-days because PROs don't seem to be about this, but if you want to do it right, you have to:*

- *Genuinely care about people*
- *Be honest and truthful*

- *Know MC history so that you can help bring about a good future for all the MCs through your work*

- *Whenever you attend an MC's function, always find the PRO and let him/her know that you are there to SUPPORT that MC! Not, I've attended your party—so I know I'll be seeing ya'll at ours... It shouldn't matter whether or not they ever come to your function. You are there to support them so they can grow.*

- *PROs walk up to folks all the time at a party and hand someone their flyer. "Hey come to our party." When they walk away they leave you thinking, "I don't know this person. I know nothing about their MC. They didn't even try to build a relationship! Yeah right, I ain't going to their party." Then you throw the flyer on the ground."*

Black Dragon: *"So, PROs should be relationship builders? You seem to know a lot about it. Why aren't you a PRO any longer?"*

S.A.T: *"I will never be a PRO again Dragon. It is my opinion that the position has become corrupt in today's MC environment. It has been taken over by very selfish people. Today's PRO seems to be all about seeing how they can use others to get what they need or want them to do to support their club's agenda—rather than because they have a genuine interest in seeing all MC's prevail, flourish, and thrive."*

◊◊◊

Getting out Early on the Event

Perhaps one of the biggest lessons I can teach PROs about the whole annual planning thing is to GET IT OUT EARLY!!! Some 'ORGANIZED' MCs have their yearly calendar planned over one year out. They know what parties they are going to and everything. If you wait until two months before your party to start marketing and advertising your party, chances are, it will not be well attended. I know some MCs that are getting their party flyers out nearly a year in advance! At the very least, it should be six months in advance. There is a PR plan development sheet in the PR Tips chapter you can use to help you in timing and delivery. This also goes for poker runs, rides, or other projects, there can never be enough said about how important it is to get the information out in front of the event far enough for invitees to have enough time to plan to attend. The fact is that last minute events are seldom well attended. In today's MC environment, because there are thousands more MCs than there ever were, there are too many competing events out there to expect that your last minute event will yield satisfactory attendance results.

Here are some tips:

The MC has the goal of getting the event planned and worked out, getting the money together to run the event, and securing the event location and facilities. In a perfect world, the MC will take care of these details in plenty of time. This makes the Professional Communicator's job easy. However, all of these pieces often may not come together until the last minute given the planners in the MC may not be as organized. So, what is the Professional Communicator to do?

1. You do not have to have everything present to start getting your message out early.
2. You can put flyers out containing some of the information with messages like "time and location will be announced"

and then on a second distribution of flyers you can add the missing information.

3. Get the event out at least six months early no matter what the event is.

4. Populate your web sites, blogs, and other club Internet properties. Often, MCs update social media and fail to update their websites because it is quicker and easier to do so. Remember that folks check out your websites so update them first.

5. Engage social media. Populate Facebook, Snap Chat, Instagram, Google, and other social media pages.

◊◊◊

CHAPTER FIFTEEN
Crisis Management

As I started writing this section it just began to over flow. I could not contain it to one chapter, so I have decided to write a companion book to this one. It will be called "MC Crisis Management Bible." Until I get it out, which will be soon, I can say this about crisis management:

1. Get ahead of the crisis quickly. The press will use a statement off of your social media sites or websites before they even take the time to call you on the phone. They are trained to look for your social media sites, so if they are out there the press will find them.
2. Do not let the press speculate. Say something! Believe me, you will not like their speculation. It will always be sensational, lacking facts, and will be created with the eye towards selling advertisements and papers; not guarding the reputation of the MC.
3. Arrange a press release rather than allowing your members and officers to be picked off one by one by the press.
4. Use talking points.
5. Use backgrounder meetings to educate an aggressive police department.
6. Write Op-Eds if you need to get the MC's side of the story out.
7. Stay in your lane.

◊◊◊

Dignity and Class can be Taught and Learned

Reggie Rock Bythewood was the co-writer/Director of the Dream Works movie "Biker Boyz". When we were working together on the movie we made a decision to have a bike wash with sexy girls in once scene of the movie. I really got revved up and I started planning the scene with fervor. Reggie asked me what was on my mind.

John: "Well, man I just cannot WAIT to get started planning this scene! We are gonna have b#$@es stream in half naked with thongs up their asses, and they will actually take their tops off and begin washing the bikes, and the guys will play rap music, and the b@#$es will dance in front of the motorcycle handle bars like stripper poles........ahhhh man! Wait till I write this out!"

Reggie Rock: "Whoa, whoa! Hold on there young brotha! We are not going to do it like that, ha ha ha, what on Earth is wrong with you? We don't get down like that?"

John: "Why!!!? That's not so farfetched! I've seen things like that happen!"

Reggie Rock: "What if this is the only movie ever made in the whole world about African American lifestyles and culture on the Biker Set? What if no other movie gets made? And what if the movie gets blasted out into outer space and some civilization somewhere passed Mars beams in the broadcast? How would you have them see a representation of your people? Would you show the worst we have to offer or would you show the best we have to offer? We often complain that we don't like how others portray us yet we turn right around and play right into those some old stereotypes. Think about it brother. I'll give you one thong, and no back shots, no dancing and all tops will stay on. And you really need to stop using the "B" word."

I grew up that day. I learned that dignity, style and class comes from how you carry yourself. Believe in yourself and represent yourself before others. I have always been grateful for my big brother's lesson.

You are PRO! Guardian of the MC's reputation and manager of its publics!

Now go represent your MC with Style!

Thank you for reading my book Motorcycle Club Public Relations Officer's Bible!

John E. Bunch II

◊◊◊

Appendix A:
The PRO's Proverbs

PROs ARE IN CHARGE OF REPUTATION NOT MEMBERS
The PRO does not order members around; that is the job of other officers. The PRO merely offers timely information and a good listening ear.

Communications NOT MC Politics
The wise PRO simply funnels communications, without the slant of club politics. The PRO is a messenger of the MC's will.

What Am I Doing Right Now to Better Serve the MC?
The wise PRO asks of himself every day when he awakens, "What can I do today to better communicate the message of my MC better than I did yesterday?" Then sets out to do those things.

I Shall Document the History of the MC
Leaving the great history of a proud and noble people in the hands of others to document is harmful to the reputation of the MC. I must leave a history of the MC for the future generations because for them to ride without knowledge of those who forged their patch is shameful.

I Shall Never Filter a Message Given To Me to Deliver
I am a messenger not an interpreter.

I Shall Never Disrespect Any MC President or Other Officer
The wise PRO affords the same level of respect to President and officers of other MCs as she does her own.

I Shall Be an Ambassador of My MC

The wise PRO will tell their self, "It is my greatest hope that I bring nothing but honor and praises upon my MC. I shall conduct myself in my dealings upon the Biker Set, at all times, as an ambassador of my MC."

I Shall Surrender My Ego

The wise Pro tells himself, "I am determined to serve my MC with all that I am worth. My Full Patch brothers depend upon me. To my MC I will give my utmost!"

◊◊◊

Appendix B:
PRO's Readiness Test

After spending months or even years on the job, many PROs know absolutely nothing about the inner workings of PR and are as uninformed as the first day they took the job. This test is by no means all inclusive, but you can use it as a guide to test your overall knowledge of the job. Use it to test yourself before and after you have read *"MC PRO's Bible."*

1. What MC Officers could PROs Bible help?
2. What is the PRO's function for the MC?
3. How should the PRO's Bible be used?
4. What does the abbreviation PRO mean?
5. Where does the MC PRO position originated?
6. Why do traditional MC's claim the PRO position is invalid?
7. Why would a PRO be called a "glorified flyer dispenser"?
8. How do the traditional duties of the Secretary overlap the duties of the PRO?
9. When did the MC Professional Organization begin (month/year)?
10. What was the original name of the MC Professional Organization?
11. What was the purpose of the original meeting of the PROC?
12. How many bikers comprised the first gathering of the PROC?
13. What honed skills should a professional communicator have?
14. What duties will the PRO execute while working hand in hand with the President and Executive Committee?
15. What is reputation management?
16. What is the number one contribution of PROs to companies worldwide according to www.ProQuckStart.org?
17. What forms of media and communications do PROs use?
18. What are the working hours of an MC PRO?
19. What are the qualifications of an MC PRO?
20. What study areas can a PRO research to master their job?
21. What skills should a PRO possess to be considered for the job?

22. What are 10 case scenarios where PRO skills could be necessary?
23. Name 9 PRO tools.
24. What is a press release?
25. How is a press release used?
26. How is a press release always written?
27. What are the elements of a press release?
28. What is an analyst reference in a press release?
29. What is a customer reference in a press release?
30. What is a vendor reference in a press release?
31. What references does a level I press release contain?
32. What references does a level II press release contain?
33. What references does a level III press release contain?
34. What is the definition of a media alert?
35. What are other names for a media alert?
36. What is the order of operation in a media alert and why?
37. How does a media alert differ from a press release?
38. What are the elements of a media alert?
39. What is a press conference?
40. Name five reasons a PRO would call a press conference.
41. What are 10 good steps to carrying out a successful press conference?
42. Why does the media like interviews with VIPs?
43. What should you do if the President is becoming frustrated during a press conference?
44. How do you take over a press conference from an aggressive reporter?
45. Under what circumstances might the President only read a statement during a press conference, and answer no follow up questions at all?
46. What is a backgrounder?
47. Why is a backgrounder written?
48. Name the parts of a backgrounder.
49. How is a backgrounder disseminated?
50. What is a backgrounder meeting?
51. What does the term Op-ed mean?

52. How long should an Op-ed be?
53. When is an Op-ed used?
54. What is a bylined article?
55. How is a Letter to the Editor formatted?
56. What is the difference between a Letter to the Editor and a Fact Sheet?
57. What are the elements and purpose of a Pitch Letter?
58. When might a Pitch Letter be used?
59. Name the elements of a Media Kit.
60. What is the purpose of a Media Kit?
61. How should a Media Kit be presented?
62. How could it be useful for the MC if the PRO was a regular columnist in a magazine?
63. What is the most important tool in a media relations arsenal?
64. What does the saying "You're only as good as your list mean?"
65. What is a media list?
66. What is the best way to develop a media list?
67. What are talking points?
68. What is the purpose of talking points?
69. How can talking points be used to protect your President or officers?
70. Why is it important for general members to have talking points?
71. How can having talking points protect your MC in a case of crisis?
72. Name 12 interviewee tips.
73. Name 10 article writing tips.
74. Name 9 kinds of events that make the news.
75. Name 4 categories you can use to link your story to news relevance.
76. How does a PR plan help you promote an event?
77. How can you determine if PR can help your MC?
78. It is said that history is written by _____.
79. Why is it important to record your MC's history?
80. Who was Clifford Vaughs?
81. Who was Ben Hardy?

82. What is so difficult about getting an article published on Wikipedia?

83. Why will most MCs find it difficult to get anything positive included into a Wikipedia article?

84. Why shouldn't the press be trusted with your MC's history?

85. What is the definition of a flyer?

86. What are flyers used for?

87. Can a flyer be electronic?

88. Name four flyer sizes on printed paper?

89. What does "going two up" on a flyer mean?

90. What does flyering mean?

91. What are the 12 steps to designing flyers?

92. What can a good website design do for an MC's reputation?

93. List the 5 steps to website design.

94. How do you gather an audience once your website is built?

95. What is SEO and how does it work?

96. Why is it important to keep your MC's website updated?

97. What is social media?

98. How does social media help the MC build its reputation?

99. How can social media destroy the MC's reputation?

100. Why should the MC have good social media policies regarding members?

101. Why should you limit fan pages and MC accounts?

102. Why should you beware of who you give admin access to your sites?

103. List at least 15 things to know when planning a photo shoot.

104. What are the concerns of the MC when dealing with illness and death?

105. How can the MC help when there are missing persons from the Set?

106. What family concerns should be taken into consideration during crisis?

107. How should the PRO deal with death and burials?

108. How can the PRO's networking skills help the MC accomplish good MC to MC relations?

109. Should the PRO plan the MC's annual dances?

110. It is important to get the annual dance information out 6 months in advance. T/F

111. The PRO should be an expert at handing out flyers. T/F

112. The PRO is responsible to hand out the club flyers. T/F

113. What are 5 tips for getting information out about club events early?

◊◊◊

Appendix C: Biker Set Readiness Test

A PRO should have a firm knowledge of the MC Biker Set. Test your knowledge with the following test. This test is by no means all-inclusive but you can use it as a guide to begin your research:

1. In what city, state, and year was your MC Nation founded?
2. In what neighborhood was your MC Nation founded?
3. How many members comprised the founding fathers of your MC Nation and local chapter?
4. What were the names and occupations of the founding fathers of your MC Nation?
5. What is the motto of your MC Nation, and what does it mean?
6. How did your MC Nation obtain its first clubhouse?
7. What are the addresses of your MC Nation's mother chapter and your local chapters?
8. What is the birthday celebration of your MC Nation and all of your local chapters?
9. What is alarm code to get into the clubhouse?
10. What is mascot of your MC Nation?
11. What were the first motorcycles, makes and models, owned by the founding fathers of your MC Nation?
12. How did the founding fathers of your MC Nation learn to ride?
13. Describe your MC Nation's colors and explain the meanings, origins, and symbols of all of the elements of the patch.
14. What was the name of the first brother killed on a motorcycle in your MC Nation? What year did he die, and how was he killed?
15. Who are the racing heroes of your MC Nation? Why?
16. What is the history of the first MC split in your MC Nation and what happened to the members who split off?
17. What is the preferred bike color and style of your MC Nation?
18. How many years must you be in the MC before you are

authorized to wear the MC's colors as a tattoo?

19. What is your MC's policy for the removal of their tattoo if you should leave your MC Nation?

20. How many years must you be in the MC before you are authorized to wear the MC's medallion or ring?

21. What are the bike nights of all your MC Nation's clubhouses?

22. What are the names of the Presidents of all of the chapters within your MC Nation?

23. When did the President of your local chapter join your MC Nation? What are the telephone numbers and contact names for all of the chapters within your MC Nation?

24. How often are club meetings generally held throughout your MC Nation and when?

25. How many members are necessary to hold a quorum in your local MC?

26. What is the order procedure for how church is conducted in your MC Nation?

27. What are the monthly dues owed to the National Headquarters by all chapters in your MC Nation?

28. What are the real names, phone numbers, email addresses and emergency contact numbers for every member in your chapter?

29. What are the steps to becoming a Prospect in your MC?

30. Who can be a Prospect sponsor within your MC?

31. What are a sponsor's responsibilities?

32. When does a chapter President vote on a motion?

33. How long can your motorcycle be inoperable before you are required to buy a new one or turn in your colors?

34. What are the main responsibilities of the Road Captain?

35. Who are the Regional Presidents in your MC Nation?

36. How many miles one-way must a member ride to be recognized as a Nomad Rider in your MC Nation?

37. What are all of the award patches a rider can earn in your

MC Nation?

38. If a MC member suspects that a brother is too drunk to ride what is their obligation to that drunken member according to your MC's bylaws or policies?

39. What is the MC's procedure for one member borrowing money from another member?

40. What is the procedure for solving a physical altercation between two members in your MC Nation?

41. What member of your MC is allowed to physically strike another other member?

42. What members in a local chapter can actually fine other members?

43. What members in your local chapter can actually fine the chapter President?

44. Under what specific circumstances may your colors be taken from you for an infraction against the bylaws?

45. If a local chapter president requests your colors what must be done before the president can keep your colors forever?

46. Who comprises your MC's governing Council?

47. Is your MC coed?

48. What can your wife or girlfriend wear to support the MC if she is not a member?

49. What is the status of women associated with your MC?

50. Does your MC have a First Lady and if so who is she?

51. What is the definition of a member in good standing?

52. What are the main responsibilities of a Prospect within your MC Nation?

53. What are the basic rules of conduct for a Prospect within your MC Nation?

54. Where are required patches to be worn on the vest of a Prospect and full patched brothers?

55. What is the quickest way to tell if you are dealing with a 1% outlaw MC Nation member if you greet him face to face and have not seen the back of his vest?

56. How can you distinguish outlaw colors from the back?

57. What is the definition of an Outlaw MC?

58. What is a 99%er MC?

59. What is a 1%er MC?

60. Is there a difference between an outlaw MC and a 1%er MC and if so what is that difference?

61. Where did the term 1%er come from?

62. What is the philosophical definition that sets 1% MCs apart from traditional MCs?

63. Who was the first person to lose his life in a clubhouse altercation within your MC Nation?

64. What criminal or civil actions, if any, have been brought against your local or national MC by city, local, or national law enforcement agencies in an attempt to shut down, prosecute, and/or fine your MC during its history, and what were the outcomes of those charges?

65. What were the lessons learned from question 64?

66. What were the names of any members that have been murdered or accosted while representing your MC Nation?

67. What caused any second or subsequent MC splits within your MC Nation?

68. To whom do the colors, insignia, designs, patches, logos, and other paraphernalia of your MC belong?

69. How many MCs has your MC Nation flipped or patched over, and to what MC Nation did those chapters belong before they were flipped/patched over?

70. Does your MC Nation wear support patches for a 1%er MC Nation? If so, which one?

71. If your MC Nation wears support patches for a 1%er MC Nation, who are their enemies?

72. If your MC Nation wears support patches what areas of town, cities, or states is it unsafe for you to ride in your colors without being in the company of your brothers?

73. Why is it important to always remember that you are representing every MC member within your Nation when

you are operating out in public?

74. What is your MC's consequence to you if you rip your patch off of your vest?
75. What is the consequence for striking another brother of your MC?
76. What is the consequence for stealing from your MC?
77. What is the consequence for discussing MC business outside of the MC?
78. What is the consequence for posting MC business on social media?
79. What is the consequence for cyber-banging on social media?
80. What is the consequence for losing your colors?
81. What is the consequence for disrespecting your colors?
82. Should your colors ever touch the ground?
83. Should you ever let anyone outside of your MC hold your colors?
84. What is another term for the vest used to hold your colors?
85. What does the term backyard mean?
86. What is the 80/20 rule?
87. What is the AMA?
88. What is ABATE?
89. What is a boneyard?
90. What are broken wings?
91. Why is it against protocol to burnout in front of another MC's clubhouse?
92. What is a cage?
93. What is the rule about wearing your vest in a cage?
94. What does going to church mean in the MC world?
95. What is the proper procedure for dating the property of a 1%er MC?
96. What is the biggest no-no about parking in front of another MC's clubhouse?
97. What happens if you put your helmet on the bar of a MC you are visiting?

98. What does the term "Club Hopping" mean?

99. If your President wants to Prospect a hang-around who was first a member of another MC, what is the proper protocol to accomplish this?

100. What is the proper protocol for approaching a girl with another MC's patch on her back to ask her to dance or go out?

101. What is the proper protocol for passing an outlaw or senior MC on the open highway when your pack is traveling faster than theirs?

102. What does counter steering mean and how is it done?

103. To what does the term "Slow, Look, Lean, and Roll" refer?

104. What is the proper hand signal to flash to the pack when a cop/highway patrol vehicle is spotted?

105. What is the proper hand signal flashed to the pack when debris is in the road on the left side of the bike?

106. What is the proper foot signal flashed to the pack when debris is in the road on the right side of the bike?

107. What is the proper hand signal flashed when the Road Captain wants the pack to assume a single file formation?

108. What is the proper hand signal flashed when the Road Captain wants the pack to assume a staggered formation?

109. What is the proper hand signal flashed when the Road Captain wants the pack to assume the suicide (two abreast) formation?

110. When the Road Captain lifts his hand up to indicate a left or right turn what does the rest of the pack do?

111. What is the proper hand signal flashed when the Road Captain wants the pack to slow down?

112. What is the proper hand signal flashed when the Road Captain wants the pack to continue on while he drops out of the pack to view it for safety?

113. What is the proper hand signal flashed when the Road Captain wishes to change places with the Assistant Road Captain in the back of the pack?

114. What is the best way to cross railroad tracks in an intersection?
115. During a rain storm when is the road the slickest?
116. When braking a motorcycle, what is meant by the term "reaction time?"
117. When traveling twenty mph how many feet does it take to bring a motorcycle to a complete stop including reaction time?
118. When traveling 80 mph how many feet does it take to bring a motorcycle to a complete stop including reaction time?
119. Why does the front brake have more braking power than the rear brake?
120. According to distribution of impact locations on motorcycle helmets during collision studies conducted by Dietmar Otte, Medizinische Hochschule Hannover, and Abteilung Verkehrsunfallforschung in Germany, where are most head injuries concentrated for motorcyclists?
121. What does DOT stand for and why is it important when purchasing a motorcycle helmet?
122. What is a flash patch?
123. What is a freedom fighter?
124. What does FTW mean?
125. What does KTRSD mean?
126. What does LE/LO mean?
127. What is an OMC?
128. What is an OMG?
129. Are cell phones allowed in your church meetings?
130. What is the consequence for secretly taping your church meetings?
131. What is an MRO?
132. What does the term "On Ground" mean?
133. What does the term "On Two" mean?
134. What does the term "Patch Over" mean?
135. What does the term "Flipping" mean?
136. What is a PRO?
137. What is a probie?

138. What are the major differences between an RC and a MC?

139. What is the RICO act?

140. What is a rocker?

141. What is a run?

142. What is a gypsy run?

143. What is special about a mandatory run?

144. What is a tail gunner?

145. What does the diamond "13" mean?

146. What is the significance of the three-piece patch?

147. What is the significance of turning your back on another MC or patched person?

148. What does BSFFBS mean?

149. What does DILLIGAF mean?

150. What is a 5%er?

151. What is a lick and stick?

152. What does the term "Running 66" mean?

153. What is a vested pedestrian?

154. What is a hang-around?

155. What is a civilian?

156. What is a "Property of"?

157. What is a House Mamma?

158. What is an ink slinger?

159. How often should the financial report be given at your MC's club meeting?

160. Where must your MC's colors be purchased?

161. What are your rights if you ever face your MC's disciplinary committee?

162. What is necessary for you to be found guilty of a charge in your MC?

163. Who are the closest MCs to your MC Nation who can be considered to love your MC like brothers and where your MC will always have a home away from home (allies)?

164. What is a dominate MC?

165. It is possible to Prospect for your MC without owning a motorcycle?

166. If you don't like the direction your MC pack is going you can simply leave the pack and take a shortcut and catch up to the pack later? Y/N

167. Folks can join your MC without prospecting? T/F

168. It is okay to pop a wheelie in the pack? T/F

169. It is okay to leave a brother in trouble? T/F

170. It is okay to screw a brother's old lady or wife? T/F

171. Can the Road Captain fine a member without a trial for infractions committed in the pack?

172. When can the Road Captain order a member not to ride their bike?

173. Does the Road Captain have the right to see a member's license, registration and insurance in your MC?

174. When is it okay to give out personal information about a MC member to someone outside of the MC?

175. It is okay for an MC President to attend a function thrown by your MC without being searched for a weapon if everyone else is being searched?

176. What is the ranking order for the way your MC rides in formation?

177. Where does a Prospect ride when escorting a senior member of the MC Nation?

178. What is the first responsibility a Prospect is assigned after he learns to ride in the pack?

179. What is 'packing', and is a Prospect ever allowed to pack?

180. Who was the first Godfather of your MC Nation, and what was his contribution to the MC?

181. When did the original Godfather die?

182. Who is the Godfather of your MC Nation today?

183. When is the Road Captain considered the President of a local chapter?

184. What is required to take a leave of absence from your MC?

185. When are you allowed to retire from your MC?

186. Where are standard business cards ordered?

187. What is the email address of any MC member in the nation?

188. How do you get a MC email address?

189. What duties must a Prospect perform daily in your chapter?

190. Can a Prospect crossover without speaking with the National President, National VP or the High Council President in your MC Nation?

191. What is the name of the most honored veteran within your MC Nation?

192. When was the office of National President created within your MC Nation?

193. How many MCs operate in your town and what are the names of twenty-five of them?

194. What is the C.O.C.?

195. What is meant by the term "Top 5" when talking about MCs?

196.

197. Name the OMCs in every state surrounding yours.

198. What is a supporter MC?

199. It is okay to walk into a MC representing your MC Nation without wearing your colors?

200. Should you have a Set of colors with you no matter where you travel?

201. What is the mission statement of your MC Nation?

202. Does handling a problem internally within the MC relive you of your legal responsibility to call law enforcement if you think a crime has been committed?

203. What are the rules for all members to stand duty at the clubhouse should your chapter have a clubhouse?

204. What are your MC's national and local website addresses?

205. Does your MC have a women's auxiliary?

206. Does your MC have a Support Crew?

207. What is the phone number and password used for your MC's conference calls?

208. How do you jump start a motorcycle?

209. When would you jump start a motorcycle?

210. Can you use a car to jump start a motorcycle safely?

211. How can one battery man on a motorcycle push another man on a motorcycle without a strap or rope or chain?

212. How do you pick up a heavy motorcycle like a Gold Wing or a Hog if it falls over and you are by yourself?

213. Does your MC ride in staggered or suicide formation?

214. Where is lane splitting legal in the United States?

215. When encountering a tornado on the open road should you take refuge under a bridge? Why or why not? (Refer to http://www.srh.noaa.gov/oun/?n=safety-overpass, especially slide 22 – this may save your life!)

216. What should be done to avoid tornadoes in open country?

217. If riding on the open highway and you encounter sudden heavy fog how should you seek to protect yourself?

218. When riding across country in extreme heat (100° F or higher) degrees what is one of your greatest mechanical concerns?

219. When riding across country in extreme heat (100° F or higher) degrees how can you quickly cool off if you feel overwhelmed by the heat?

220. When traveling cross country through various OMC territories what should your MC do before entering their territory?

221. If riding cross country what auto parts store will always carry motorcycle batteries?

222. How does the AAA 'club motorcycle towing package' differ from your motorcycle insurance coverage towing plan?

223. When riding with another MC, where should your MC pack be located?

224. What is your local chapter's responsibility to your MC Nation?

225. If your MC chapter needs a bank account is it okay for a member to put that account in his name?

226. What is the purpose of the website
www.praying24hours.com?

227. Why do you want to be a member of your MC Nation?

228. What do you bring to your MC Nation?

229. What do you want from your MC Nation?

◊◊◊

Appendix D:
Brief History of the
Mighty Black Sabbath Motorcycle Club Nation

Mighty Black Sabbath Motorcycle Club Nation

The Mighty Black Sabbath Motorcycle Club Nation is a national, traditional 99%er law abiding motorcycle club whose members ride all makes of street legal motorcycles (cruisers at least 750cc and sport bikes at least 600cc). The Mighty Black Sabbath Motorcycle Club Nation does not belong to any governing organizations like the

AMA but is law abiding and is not a 1%er Outlaw MC Nation. It is not listed by the United States Department of Justice or any other law enforcement organizations as an OMC or an OMG. The Black Sabbath MC derived its name from the actions of the Original Seven African American male founders who rode on Sundays after church. When the Original Seven were looking for a name to call themselves—they said, "We are seven black men who ride on the Sabbath day after worship, so let's call ourselves Black Sabbath!"

History

The Original Seven founding fathers of the Black Sabbath Motorcycle Club Nation taught themselves to ride on one Honda 305 Scrambler in the hills of a neighborhood called Mount Hope in San Diego, California in 1972. That bike, given to 'Pep' by a close friend, was shared between them. The founding fathers mostly worked at the San Diego Gas and Electric Company or were enlisted in the US Navy. They practiced evenings and weekends on the Honda 305 Scrambler, until they eventually learned how to ride and each bought a motorcycle.

Faithfully, they gathered at each other's garages after church on Sundays to ride, tell tall tales, and drink beers. By 1974, their wives united and revolted, demanding that no more club meetings be held in their garages on Sundays because the neighbors kept complaining and the wives felt threatened by the strength of the brotherhood. Undaunted, the founding fathers rented an abandoned bar at 4280 Market Street; where they remained one of the most dominant, influential, and successful MCs on the African American Biker Set since 1974 (over forty years at the time of this writing). The brothers got their colors blessed by the Chosen Few MC Nation and the Hells Angels MC Nation in February 1974 after getting their clubhouse.

Founding Fathers

The seven original founding fathers were:
- First Rider: Robert D. Hubbard 'Sir Hub' (SDG&E Electrician)
- VP: William Charles Sanders 'Couchie'(SDG&E Electrician)

- Sgt-at-Arms Alvin Ray 'Stretch'
- Road Capt: Paul Perry 'Pep' (SDG&E Meter Reader)
- Asst Road: Capt: Solomon 'Sol'
- Secretary: John Kearny 'Black'
- Unnamed brother whose name has been lost to us

Racing roots

The Black Sabbath MC was not complicated in its mission during the early years. It was comprised simply of seven men who loved to ride, mostly on Sundays, who were similarly possessed with an insatiable appetite for custom building "Choppers" and unbeatable drag race bikes. This is still true today. All bike styles are welcomed and racers are most cherished in the Mighty Black Sabbath Motorcycle Club Nation.

Battle cry "I came to race"

The MC's battle cry was fathered by Black Sabbath MC legend-fabled racer, Allen 'Sugar Man' Brooks, who once wrecked Pep's motorcycle (early 1970's) at the Salton Sea bike run/race event without a helmet, at over one hundred ten mph. Pep had warned Sugar Man that his bike was not operating properly and was excessively vibrating when it got to one hundred mph. Sugar Man still insisted that Pep let him test it. Needless to say, he exceeded one hundred mph and destroyed Pep's bike. After the accident, Sugar Man was forbidden to compete as the MC deemed that he was too injured to race. The President threatened to take his colors if he attempted to drag race the next day. Sugar Man said, "You can take these damned colors if you will. I came to race!" Sugar Man consequently won the drag racing competition despite his injuries; thereby etching himself into the Black Sabbath MC's history books.

San Diego Mother Chapter

The Mighty Black Sabbath Motorcycle Club Nation's mother chapter clubhouse stood at 4280 Market Street on the corner for forty years. During most of that time the MC reined dominant as the most successful MC in San Diego and is the oldest surviving MC on the black Biker Set in San Diego. For decades, the Black Sabbath MC clubhouse was the only clubhouse on the black Biker Set. During that time, all San Diego and Los Angeles MCs came to San Diego to celebrate the Sabbath's yearly anniversary, which was the first run of the year. Even to this day, West Coast MCs gather in San Diego for the first run of the year established by the Black Sabbath MC.

Nationwide chapters

The Mighty Black Sabbath Motorcycle Club Nation has chapters across the United States from coast to coast. Growth was initially slow as the MC never envisioned itself a national MC from its inception in San Diego in 1974. The Black Sabbath MC is the oldest surviving MC born in San Diego. The second charter was not given until 1989 some fifteen years after the MC started. Club racing legend, Allen 'Sugar Man' Brooks, took the colors to Wichita, Kansas where Knight Rider and Lady Magic (previously members of the Penguins MC) developed the chapter; subsequently becoming the oldest surviving MC on the black Biker Set in that city.

In 1999, then National President Pep, launched the Denver, Colorado chapter. Not long after, he assigned veteran member, Leonard Mack, to head up the Minneapolis, Minnesota chapter. Two years later, Dirty Red launched the St. Paul, Minnesota chapter. In 2004, Pep launched the Little Rock, Arkansas chapter with his nephew, Lewis 'Doc' Perry, who became the first East Coast Regional President. Once again, two years later Doc launched the Oklahoma City, Oklahoma chapter with his high school buddy, James 'JB' Baker, as President. In 2008, National Ambassador and former mother chapter President, Dewey 'Jazz' Johnson, launched the Phoenix, Arizona chapter. By then, the Wichita, Kansas chapter was all but dead.

Exponential growth was not seen until 2009 when then National Enforcer John E. 'Black Dragon' Bunch II convinced Sugar Man to come out of retirement and launch the Tulsa, Oklahoma chapter. Black Dragon reopened the Wichita, Kansas chapter using hard core recruiting efforts but could not sustain the re-launch until Lady Magic tapped her son, 'Pull-it', and grandson, Chris 'Chill' Hill, to restart Wichita. Black Dragon simultaneously launched the Atlanta, Georgia chapter with former Oklahoma City member, Pappy, who had also grown up with Doc Perry. Later, in 2009, Black Dragon launched the Houston, Texas chapter with Bernard 'Krow'Augustus who became the first Midwest/Central USA Regional President.

In 2010, the Atlanta, Georgia chapter was taken over by Black Dragon's former submarine shipmate, Leon 'Eight Ball' Richardson, who also became the first East Coast Regional President. Black Dragon became National President in 2010, and patched over the Macon, Georgia chapter under Curtis 'Ride or Die' Hill, who became the third East Coast Regional President. Black Dragon then patched-over the Sic Wit' It MC in Rome, Georgia under President G Man.

Sugar Man's first cousin, Jamel 'Huggy Bear' Brooks, launched the San Antonio, Texas chapter by the end of 2010, and became the first West Coast Regional President assuming command of the Phoenix, Arizona chapter. Huggy Bear patched over the Inland Empire, California chapter under the leadership of Big Dale in 2011. Big Dale eventually became the second West Coast Regional President. In 2012, National Vice President Tommy 'Hog Man' Lewis received a blessing from the Chosen Few MC to open the Las Vegas, Nevada chapter with then West Coast Regional President Huggy Bear. In 2012, the Jacksonville, Florida chapter was launched under President Prime. In 2014, the West Coast Regional President Big Dale launched the Riverside, California chapter under President Bob O. In 2015, the Hutchinson, Kansas chapter opened under the flag, "West Wichita", under President Dizzle. The Colorado Springs, Colorado chapter was launched under President G-Ride; and so it went: the Beaufort, South Carolina chapter was launched under President Homesick, the Pensacola, Florida chapter was launched under President OlSkool, and the Fort Worth, Texas chapter was launched under President Big Mixx. At the time of this writing, there are seven more prospective Black Sabbath MC chapters seeking to gain entry. Hail to the forefathers of the Mighty Black Sabbath Motorcycle Club Nation! We hope they are proud of what their dreams have become. Amen.

Membership

A prospective member is allowed into the Black Sabbath Motorcycle Club as a "hang-around," indicating that the individual is invited to some MC events or to meet MC members at known gathering places. This period could last several months to several years. It is the time for the hang-around to evaluate the MC, as well as for the MC to evaluate the hang-around. If the hang-around is interested, and the Black Sabbath Motorcycle Club likes the hang-around; he can request to be voted in as a Prospect. The hang-around must win a majority vote to be designated a Prospect. If he is successful he will be given a sponsor and his prospectship begins. The prospectship will be no less than ninety days, but could last for years, depending upon the attitude and resourcefulness of the Prospect. National President Black Dragon prospected for nearly five years before he was accepted. The Prospect will participate in some MC activities, and serve the MC in whatever capacity the full patched brothers may deem appropriate. A Prospect will never be asked to commit any illegal act, any act against nature, or any physically humiliating or demeaning act. The Black Sabbath Motorcycle Club never hazes Prospects. A Prospect will not have voting privileges while he is evaluated for suitability as a full member but does pay MC dues.

The last phase, and highest membership status, is "Full Membership" or "Full-Patch". The term "Full-Patch" refers to the complete one-piece patch. Prospects are allowed to wear only a small thirteen-inch patch with the letters of the local chapter (i.e. BSSD) and the black cross on it. To become a full patched brother the Prospect must be presented by his sponsor before the MC and win a one hundred percent affirmative vote from the full patched brothers. Prior to votes being cast, a Prospect usually travels to every chapter in the sponsoring chapter's geographic region (state/province/territory) and introduces himself to every full patched brother. This process allows all regional chapter members to become familiar with the Prospect. Some form of formal induction follows, wherein the Prospect affirms his loyalty to the MC and its members. Often the Prospect's sponsor may require him to make a nomadic journey on his motorcycle before crossing over, sometimes as far as 1,000 miles that must be completed within twenty-four hours to ensure that the Prospect understands the Black Sabbath Motorcycle Club is a riding motorcycle club. The final logo patch is then awarded at his swearing in and initiation ceremony. The step of attaining full membership can be referred to as "being patched", "patching in" or "crossing over."

Command Structure
- National President
- National Vice President
- High Council President
- High Council
- National Business Manager
- National Ambassador
- Regional President
- President
- Vice President
- Secretary
- Sgt-at-Arms
- Road Captain
- Treasurer
- Business Manager
- Public Relations Officer
- Media/Web Design Officer
- Full Patch Member
- First Lady S.O.T.C.
- Full Patch S.O.T.C.
- Head Goddess
- Full Patch Goddess

- Support Crew
- Prospect
- S.O.T.C. Prospect
- Goddess Prospect
- Hang Around
- Special officers include Disaster Chief, Nomad, National Sgt-at-Arms, Enforcer, Support Crew Chief, Godfather and Godmother.

Colors

The Black Sabbath Motorcycle Club patch is called the "Turtle Shell". The colors are set out on a white background inside a black circle, inside a black crested shield, with the words Black Sabbath MC encircling the riding man. The crested shield on the sixteen-inch back patch gives the appearance of a turtle's shell when worn as it covers most members' entire back. The MC's colors are white, yellow, black and blue.

In the forty-plus year history of the MC the colors have remained untouched except for the addition of the shield in 1975 and the enlargement of the patch to nineteen-inch by sixteen inch in 2009. The adherence to the original patch mirrors their adherence to the core values of the Original Seven founding forefathers.

Since the Black Sabbath Motorcycle Club does not claim territory like dominant 1%er MC Nations its members do not wear state bottom rockers. The cities of the chapters are named on the colors.

Racial Policies

Because the Black Sabbath Motorcycle Club was started by African Americans and its membership is primarily African American (90%) it is considered to be on the 'Black Biker Set" by biker clubs across America. However, the Black Sabbath Motorcycle Club states that even though it was started by seven African American men who rode on Sundays, today it is a multi-racial organization that is accepting of all religions, with chapters across the United States from coast to coast. The Mighty Black Sabbath Motorcycle Club Nation is a brotherhood based on a unified lifestyle centered on riding motorcycles, living the biker lifestyle, and embracing one another as extended family- as close as any blood relatives.

Neutrality

The Mighty Black Sabbath Motorcycle Club Nation has followed all MC protocol in setting up its chapters nationwide. To that end, it has received blessings to operate by dominants in every area in which it has chapters. As a neutral 99%er elite motorcycle-enthusiast riding MC the Mighty Black Sabbath Motorcycle Club Nation wears no support patches as it takes no political sides and does not align itself with OMC politics.

Women in the Black Sabbath MC Nation

A male dominated organization, the Mighty Black Sabbath Motorcycle Club Nation men belong to the brotherhood of the cross. Women fall into two unique categories. Women who do not ride motorcycles belong to the female support social club known as "Goddesses of the Mighty Black Sabbath Motorcycle Club Nation". Women who ride motorcycles belong to the "Sisters of the Cross MC of the Mighty Black Sabbath Motorcycle Club Nation".

Sisters of the Cross

The Sisters of the Cross MC of the Mighty Black Sabbath Motorcycle Club Nation (SOTC) is a female motorcycle club that rides under the full patched brothers of the Black Sabbath Motorcycle Club. The SOTC was established in 2011 by National President, Black Dragon. SOTC Prospects must be eighteen years old, own a motorcycle and have a motorcycle driver's license. The SOTC are called the "First Ladies of the Black Sabbath Motorcycle Club", and the ranking SOTC is called First Lady. The SOTC MC was created to recognize the achievements of many of the Goddesses of the Black Sabbath Motorcycle Club who were buying, learning how to ride, and getting licenses for motorcycles at an incredible rate. The Mighty Black Sabbath Motorcycle Club Nation sought to reward the hard work and passion to ride these women displayed by giving them their own MC under the auspices of the Mighty Black Sabbath Motorcycle Club Nation.

Goddesses of the Club

The Goddesses of the Mighty Black Sabbath Motorcycle Club Nation is the social club auxiliary that supports the MC. Goddess Prospects must be eighteen years old, be of exceptional character and devoted to serve the best interests of the Mighty Black Sabbath Motorcycle Club.

Mission Statement

1. "To become the greatest riding motorcycle club in the world by pounding down great distances on two wheels, bonding on the highways and byways as family, camping out while riding to biker events or cross country, enjoying the wilderness, racing, competing, winning, and experiencing our extended family by tenderly loving each other more and more each day!

2. To become the greatest motorcycle club family in the world by encouraging diversity within our MC, building strong, lasting friendships among members, instilling a sense of love, pride, and togetherness within our communities, helping those in need through volunteerism, and cultivating a mindset of moral and social responsibility amongst our members; also, by inspiring our youth to achieve beyond all limitations which will leave a legacy of hope and boundless dreams for future generations of the Mighty Black Sabbath Motorcycle Club Nation to come."

National President

The office of the National President was created by Tommy 'Hog Man' Lewis then President of the mother chapter and former mother chapter President Dewey 'Jazz' Johnson in the summer of 2000. Paul 'Pep' Perry, the last original founding member left in the chapter, was elected the first National President. Curtis 'Mad Mitch' Mitchell was appointed first National Vice President one year later. Pep also created the office of National Ambassador to which he assigned Jazz. The National Vice President position was eventually terminated. In 2010, Godfather Washington of the Mighty Black Sabbath Motorcycle Club Nation died and Pep retired to become Godfather. National Enforcer and President of the Atlanta chapter, Black Dragon, was summoned to the mother chapter in San Diego and was elected as the second National President of the Might Black Sabbath Motorcycle Club Nation during the February mother chapter annual dance. Black Dragon recreated the National Vice

President office and recruited then retired former San Diego President Hog Man for the position. Black Dragon created the High Council President office to which he assigned Sabbath racing legend Sugar Man. He also created the High Council which consists of the President and Vice President of every chapter. Black Dragon also created the National Sgt-at-Arms, National Business Manager, Nomad, Disaster Chief, Support Chief, and PRO offices.

Riding Awards and Designations

In order to challenge his MC members to ride harder and to distinguish the Mighty Black Sabbath Motorcycle Club Nation as a superior elite motorcycle-enthusiast riding MC, Black Dragon created the Nomad Rider program. In an article written in the Black Sabbath Magazine, Black Dragon stated, "A 99%er law abiding MC Nation is nothing if its members do not ride!" The Nomad Rider program recognizes and awards Black Sabbath Motorcycle Club nomad riders for their achievements. Some of the awards include:

- Nomad Rider = 1,000 miles one-way (N1)
- 1 K in 1 Day Nomad = 1,000 miles one-way ridden in twenty-four hours or less (N124)
- Nomad Traveler = 2,000 miles one-way (N2)
- Nomad Warrior = 3,000 miles one-way (N3)
- Nomad Adventurer = 4,000 miles one-way (N4)
- Nomad Wanderer = 5,000 miles one-way (N5)
- Snow Bear Disciple Nomad = one hundred miles traveled in sleet, snow, or 18° F (SBN)
- Poseidon's Disciples Nomad = traveling through three states during continuous driving rain (PSN)
- Great Plains Nomad = riding across the Oklahoma or Kansas great plains (GPN)
- Panhandle Nomad = riding across the great state of Texas (TPN)
- Great Winds Nomad = riding through fifty mph wind storm (GWN)
- 1,000 mile bull's horn = eleven inch bull's blowing horn, awarded to all Nomad Riders

- 2,000 mile Kudu's horn shofar = twenty-three inch Kudu antelope's blowing horn, awarded to all Nomad Travelers
- 3,000 mile Kudu's horn shofar = thirty-three inch Kudu or Blesbok antelope's blowing horn, awarded to all Nomad Warriors
- 4,000 mile horn shofar = forty inch Kudu, Blesbok or Impala antelope's blowing horn, awarded to all Nomad Adventurers; can be Kudu, Blesbok or Impala
- 5,000 mile horn shofar = fifty inch antelope's blowing horn, awarded to all Nomad Wanderers; can be any horned cloven footed animal.

Violence

Violent incidents have occurred in and around nationwide clubhouses.

- In 2002, President 'Bull' of the Zodiacs MC was killed after he pulled a gun on his former Prospect, who was partying at the mother chapter with a new MC in which he was interested. The former Prospect slashed Bull's throat with a knife when he looked away during the confrontation. This was the first killing ever committed at a Black Sabbath MC clubhouse, and brought the city of San Diego down on top of the clubhouse. The City Attorney initiated a campaign to shut down the clubhouse nearly finishing the Black Sabbath MC. The clubhouse was subsequently firebombed in retaliation for Bull's killing.

- In February 2010, the mother chapter at 4280 Market Street was again targeted by arsonists who attempted to burn it to the ground right before the 2010 annual. They were unsuccessful.

- In 2010, a man was fatally shot in a hail of gunfire outside the Phoenix chapter of the Black Sabbath MC clubhouse during an altercation over a woman. He died a block away while fleeing the scene. This incident caused the closing of the Phoenix chapter clubhouse.

- On 11 May 2012, San Diego mother chapter President, 'Wild Dogg', was murdered in front of the Black Sabbath Motorcycle Club clubhouse at 4280 Market Street during a drive by assassination.

The case is still unsolved and open.

Epilogue
"Everything that I stand so firmly against today, I once was! It is only through experience, pain, suffering, and being blessed to learn life's lessons that I have evolved to whom I've become. "
John E. Bunch II

◊◊◊

Glossary

1%er: Initially a description falsely attributed to the AMA to describe some of the MCs that attended Rolling Gypsy race meets. It was alleged that the AMA stated that 99% of the people at their events were God fearing and family oriented. The other 1% were hoodlums, thugs and outlaws. Non-AMA sanctioned MCs, thus being seen as outlaws, adopted the 1%er moniker and embraced it as an identity. Over time the 1%er designation became exclusively associated with OMGs, criminal biker syndicates, and some OMCs. Though not all 1%ers are criminals it is certain that the 1% diamond designation attracts law enforcement scrutiny like no other symbol on a biker's cut.

5%er: A member of a MRO. Only five percent of motorcyclists are involved with MROs that are dedicated to protecting the rights of the other ninety-five percent of bikers by spending money, dedicating time, and championing pro-biker legislation.

80/20 Rule: A requirement held by some MC councils requiring all blessed MCs within a council's region to demonstrate, via a bike count, that 80% of the MC's members have operational motorcycles at all times.

AMA: American Motorcyclist Association

ABATE: An organization started by Easy Rider Magazine to fight against discrimination toward motorcyclists, mostly helmet laws originally. Once called "A Brotherhood Against Totalitarian Enactments" or "American Bikers Against Totalitarian Enactments", ABATE now has many other names including "American Brotherhood (or Bikers) Aimed Toward Education". ABATE fights for biker rights and champions many issues well beyond helmet laws. Members often help charities. Membership comes with yearly dues and officers are elected from the active membership.

Ape Hangers: Tall handlebars that place a biker's hands at or above his shoulder height

Backyard: Where you ride often—never defecate there.

Baffle: Sound deadening material inside a muffler that quiets the exhaust noises.

Bike Count: To stem the tide of the so called "popup clubs" some councils require a minimum number of motorcycles to be in a MC before they will allow it to start up in their region. MC numbers are proven when the MC undergoes a bike count of its members; usually with all members present on their bikes.

Black Ball List: A list enacted by a MC coalition or council. It is directed at non-compliant MCs that serve to notify other MCs not to support the "black-balled" chapter nor allow it to participate in any coalition authorized Set functions.

Blockhead: The V-twin engine Harley, 1984 - 2000

Boneyard: Salvage yard for used bikes and parts

Brain Bucket: Small, beanie-style helmet (usually not Department of Transportation (DOT) approved).

Broad: A female entertainer for the MC. She may be a dancer or at times a prostitute.

Broken Wings: A patch meaning the rider has been in a crash.

Burnout: Spinning the rear wheel while holding the front brake. (Conducting burnouts while visiting another MC's clubhouse is disrespectful as it brings complaints from the neighborhood and invites unwanted police attention. Make trouble in your own neighborhood and be respectful with noise and other commotion while visiting others.)

Cage: Any vehicle of four or more wheels, specifically not a motorcycle.

Cager: Driver of a cage. (Usually cagers are thought of as dangerous to bikers because they do not pay attention to the road.)

Chopper: A bike with the front end raked or extended out.

Chromeitis: A disease associated with a biker that can't seem to buy enough aftermarket accessories (especially chrome).

Church: Clubhouse ("Having church" or "going to church" is referred to as the club meeting at the clubhouse).

CLAP: Chrome, Leather, Accessories, Performance

Clone: A motorcycle built to resemble and function like a Harley-Davidson motorcycle without actually being a Harley-Davidson motorcycle.

Club Name: Also known as a "Handle". A name given to a MC member by his brothers most often based upon his character, routine, quirks, and/or a noteworthy event that happened in the MC of which that member played a part. This is usually a name of honor and often indicates the personality one might expect when encountering that member (i.e., 'Bad Ass'). This name is generally accepted with great pride by the member and is a handle he will adopt for a lifetime. For instance, I once became annoyed with a member of the Black Sabbath Atlanta chapter for giving me a hard time when I needed him to break into my house and get the keys to my trailer so he could rescue me from the side of the road in Little Rock, AR nine hours away. He gave me so much grief about my trailer registration, working condition of my signal lights, and notifying authorities before he would break in my place that I frustratingly named him "By-the-Book", instantly changing his name from "Glock." By-the-Book so loved his new name that when he later departed the Mighty Black Sabbath M.C. Nation he took his name with him and is still called By-the-Book to this very day. (It is an honor for the MC to name you and quite improper for you to name yourself!)

Club Hopping: The frowned upon practice of switching memberships from one MC to another. Traditional MCs have low tolerance for bikers who "club hop" as this phenomenon breaks down good order and discipline in MCs. In fact, this was seldom done in the early days. Most coalitions and councils regulate club hopping and enact vigorous laws against it. Often, OMCs refuse to allow former members to wear another MC's colors after serving in their OMC. A MC should generally ensure that a club hopper waits at least six months before allowing them to Prospect for their MC unless the former President sanctions the move.

Colors: Unique motorcycle club back patch or patches

Crash Bar: Engine guard that protects the engine if the bike crashes

CreditGlide: A RUB's Motorcycle

Crotch Rocket / Rice Burner: A sport bike

Counter Steering: Turning the bike's handlebars in one direction and having it go in the opposite direction. All bikers should learn this maneuver for safety.

Custom: A custom-built motorcycle

Cut: Vest containing the MC colors. The name comes from the practice of cutting the sleeves off of blue denim jackets.

DILLIGAF: "Do I Look Like I Give A Fuck"

DOT: Department of Transportation

Drag Bars: Low, flat, straight handlebars

Evo /Evolution®: Evolution engine (V-Twin, 1984 – 2000)

Fathead: Twin-Cam engine (V-Twin, 1999 – Present)

Fender / Fender Fluff: A female passenger who is not an Old Lady but simply a lady a biker has invited for a ride.

Flathead: The Flathead engine (V-Twin, 1929 – 1972)

Flash Patch: Generic patch sold at meets and bike shops.

Flip: Occurs when an OMC takes over a less powerful OMC or 99%er. This can occur against that MC's will and could be violent. The less powerful MC will flip from their colors to the dominant MC's colors.

Flying Low: Speeding

Forward Controls: Front pegs, shifter, and rear brake control moved forward (often to the highway pegs).

Freedom Fighter: A MRO member dedicated to preserving or gaining biker's rights and freedoms.

FTA: "Fuck Them All"

FTW: "Fuck the World" or "Forever Two Wheels"

Get-Back-Whip: A two to three foot leather braid with an easy release hard metal clip that can be attached to the front break handle or the clutch handle. Often it contains a lead weight at the bottom of the braid with tassels that just barely drag the ground when the bike is standing still. This ornamental decoration can quickly be released to make a formidable weapon to be used to slap against offending cages that invade a biker's road space (to include breaking out the cager's windows). Either end can be used in an offensive or defensive situation. The Get-Back-Whip is illegal in MANY states.

Hard Tail: A motorcycle frame with no rear suspension.

Hang Around: The designation of a person who has indicated that he formally wants to get to know a MC so he can begin prospecting for them.

The Motorcycle Club Public Relations Officer's Bible

HOG: Harley Owners Group

Independent: A biker who is not a member of a MC, but is normally a well-known, accepted individual of local Biker Set (of a higher order than a hang-around).

Ink: Tattoo

Ink-Slinger: Tattoo Artist

KTRSD: "Keep the Rubber Side Down" Riding safely and keeping both tires on the road instead of up in the air—as in having a wreck.

Knuck/Knucklehead: The Knucklehead engine (V-Twin 1936 – 1947)

LE/LEO: Law Enforcement Officer/Official

Lick and Stick: A temporary pillion back seat placed on the fender through the use of suction cups.

MC: Motorcycle Club

MM: Motorcycle Ministry (Also known as 5%ers)

Moonlight Mile: A short adventure with a lady friend away from camp.

MRO: Motorcycle Rights Organization. These organizations seek to protect the rights and freedoms of bikers (i.e., ABATE, BOLT, Motorcycle Riders Foundation, American Motorcycle Association, MAG, etc.)

MSF: Motorcycle Safety Foundation

OEM: Original Equipment Manufacturer

Old / Ole Lady: Girlfriend or wife of a biker, definitely off limits!

OMC: Outlaw Motorcycle Club

OMG: Outlaw Motorcycle Gang

On Ground: Refers to showing up on or riding a motorcycle instead of showing up in or driving a cage.

On Two: Refers to showing up on or riding a motorcycle instead of showing up in or driving a cage.

Pan/Pan Head: The Pan Head engine (V-Twin, 1948 – 1965)

Patch: The back patch is the colors of a MC.

Patch-Over: Like club flipping a patch-over occurs when a MC changes patches from one MC to another. This is acceptable and not looked upon unfavorably in most cases. 99%er MCs patch-over MCs they acquire because 99%ers don't enforce territory. This will be peaceful gentlemen's agreement that happens unremarkably and without incident. 1%ers flip MCs.

Pillion Pad: Passenger Seat

Pipes: Exhaust System

PRO: Public Relations Officer

Probate/Probie/Probationary: A member serving a period of probation until he is voted into full patched (full membership) status.

Probation: The period of time a Probie must serve before full membership is bestowed. This is the time distinguished from being a hang-around because the member is voted into the Probie status and is permitted to wear some form of the MCs colors. The Probie is also responsible to follow the MC's bylaws.

Prospect: A member serving a prospectship until he is voted into full patched (full membership) status.

Prospectship: The period of time a Prospect must serve before a vote for full membership is held. This is the time distinguished from being a hang-around because the prospective member is voted into the Prospect status and permitted to wear some form of the MCs colors. The Prospect is also responsible to follow the MC's bylaws.

Rags: Club colors or a Cut.

Rat Bike: A bike that has not been maintained or loved.

RC: Riding Club. A group that rides for enjoyment (perhaps under a patch) but members do not incur the responsibility of brotherhood to the level of a traditional MCs, modern MCs or OMCs. Members generally purchase their patches and don't often Prospect/Probie to become members. Rides and runs are generally voluntarily and there is no mandatory participation. RCs are still required to follow MC protocol when operating on the MC Set and would do well to know the MC laws and respect them so as not to wind up in any kinds of altercations.

Revolution™: The Revolution engine, Harley-Davidson's first water-cooled engine (V-Twin, 2002 – Present)

RICO Act: Racketeer Influenced and Corrupt Organizations. Initially, these laws were passed for law enforcement to combat organized crime such as the mafia. They were quickly used to prosecute OMGs, OMCs, and some 99%er MCs.

Riding Bitch: Riding as the passenger on the back of a bike.

Road Name: Also known as a Handle. A name given to a MC member by his brothers and is most often based upon his character, routine, quirks, or a noteworthy event that happened in the MC of which that member played a part. This is usually a name of great honor and often indicates the personality one might expect when encountering that member (i.e. Bad Ass). This name is generally accepted with great pride by the member and is a handle he will adopt for a lifetime.

Rocker: Bottom part of MC colors which usually designates geographic location or territory, though other information may be contained there such as the word "Nomad".

RUB: Rich Urban Biker

Rubber: Tire

Rubber Side Down: Riding safely and keeping both tires on the road instead of up in the air—as in having a wreck.

Run: Road trip "on two" with your brothers.

Running 66: Though rare it is sometimes necessary to ride without the MC's colors showing (also known as "riding incognito").

Shovel/Shovel Head: The Shovel Head engine (V-Twin, 1966 – 1984)

Shower Head: The new Harley-Davidson V-Rod motorcycle motor.

Sissy Bar Passenger Backrest

Slab: Interstate

Sled: Motorcycle

Softail®: A motorcycle frame whose suspension is hidden, making it resemble a hard tail.

SMRO: State Motorcycle Rights Organization. Same as a MRO except defined by the state in which they operate, (i.e., ABATE of Oklahoma, MAG of Georgia, etc.)

Straight Pipes: An exhaust system with no Baffles

Tats: Tattoos

Tail Gunner: The last rider in the pack

The Motorcyclist Memorial Wall: A biker's memorial wall located in Hopedale Ohio where the names of fallen riders are engraved for a nominal fee (www.motorcyclistmemorial.com). Memorial bricks may also be purchased to lie at the beautiful site.

The Motorcycle Memorial Foundation: The foundation that operates the Motorcyclist Memorial Wall. P.O. Box 2573 Wintersville, Ohio 43953.

Thirteen ("13") Diamond Patch: This is a patch commonly worn by some Outlaw MC Nations. The "13" symbol can have several meanings referencing the thirteenth letter of the alphabet, "M", standing for Marijuana, Methamphetamines, Motorcycle, or the original Mother Chapter of a MC. In Hispanic gang culture, "13" can represent "La Eme" (Mexican Mafia).

Three-Piece Patch: Generally thought of as being OMC colors consisting of a top rocker (name of MC), middle insignia (MC's symbol) and bottom rocker (name of state or territory MC claims). Not only OMCs wear three piece patches but new 99%er MCs should stay away from this design and stick to a one-piece patch.

Turn your back: A show of ultimate disrespect is to turn your back on someone.

Twisties: Section of road with a lot of increasing, distal, radial turns.

Vested Pedestrian: Is a person who is in a MC and wearing colors, but does not own a motorcycle. Often thought of as a person who has never had a motorcycle, rather than someone who may be between bikes for a short period of time (i.e. a month or two).

Wannabe: Someone that tries to pretend to be a part of the biker lifestyle. (This is an excellent way to get your ass kicked!)

Wrench: Mechanic

XXF-FXX/XXFOREVER – FOREVERXX: Patch worn by MC members to represent their total commitment to the MC and every other member of that MC. XX stands for the name of the MC (i.e. Black Sabbath Forever Forever Black Sabbath).

◊◊◊

About the Author

John E. Bunch II 'Black Dragon' rode on the back of a Honda Trail 50cc for the first time when he was six years old. Instantly, he was hooked! His mother could not afford to buy him a motorcycle so he borrowed anyone's bike that would let him ride- on the back roads and farms all over Oklahoma where he grew up. When he was fourteen his mother bought him a Yamaha 125 Enduro, cashing in the US Savings Bonds his father had left him. By the time he was seventeen, his step father, J.W. Oliver, gave him a Honda CX500. He was known throughout the neighborhood as the kid who always rode wheelies up the block (16th street and Classen), and as the kid who always rode wheelies with his sisters, Thea and Lori, hanging off the back. He took his first long distance road trip at seventeen riding from Oklahoma City to Wichita, Kansas to visit his aunt and uncle. He knew then that he was born to distance ride! The nomadic call of the open road in the wind, rain, cold, heat—under the stars were home to him.

In the late 1980s, he found himself a young submarine sailor stationed in San Diego, California. He got into trouble on the base with Senior Chief who gave him and his best friend an order they refused to follow. The white Senior Chief did not want to see the young black man's career ended over insubordination so he did Bunch an extreme favor. He sent him and his insolent friend, Keith (Alcatraz) Corley, who was similarly in trouble; to see African American, then Senior Chief, George G. Clark III, instead of to a Courts Martial. Senior Chief Clark threatened Bunch and Corley with physical violence if they did not obey the white Senior Chief and worked out a solution that saved both of their careers. Later, Clark invited them to 4280 Market Street when he discovered Bunch had a love for motorcycles. Bunch walked into the mother chapter and was blown away to learn that Senior Chief Clark was also known as 'Magic', former President of the Black Sabbath Motorcycle Club Mother Chapter. His insubordinate ways were not quite behind him, so it took Bunch several years to actually cross over as a full patch brother known as 'Black Dragon' in the Black Sabbath Motorcycle Club Mother Chapter.

In 2000, Black Dragon began advising writer/filmmaker Reggie Rock Bythewood, who co-wrote and directed the Dream Works movie Biker Boyz. Black Dragon went to Hollywood and worked as the Technical Adviser on the film. Biker Boyz has often been credited with re-birthing the African American MC movement in the United States.

In 2009 Black Dragon brought the Black Sabbath Motorcycle Club to Atlanta, GA as President and an Original Seven Atlanta founding member. He suffered his first setback in Atlanta during a coupe that cost him the Presidency of the Atlanta chapter in December 2010. In February 2010, he was elected to the Office of National President and began his nationwide march to spread the Black Sabbath Motorcycle Club from coast to coast. By 2011, the Black Sabbath Motorcycle Club became the Mighty Black Sabbath

Motorcycle Club Nation with chapters from the West coast to the East coast.

Black Dragon has published several biker magazines including:

Urban Biker Cycle News, Black Iron Motorcycle Magazine, Black Sabbath Motorcycle News Letter, and the popular blog *www.blacksabbathmagazine.com.* In 2013, Black Dragon wrote the first MC phone app, *"Black Sabbath Motorcycle Club".*

Today Black Dragon is building a Mighty MC Nation that rides cross country year round, rain, sleet, or snow—where no trailers are allowed! Black Dragon and Keith 'Alcatraz' Corley currently serve the Mighty Black Sabbath Motorcycle Club Nation as brothers of the Atlanta chapter.

Black Sabbath Forever Black Sabbath
A Breed Apart
Since 1974

www.blacksabbathmc.com

◊◊◊

A NOTE FROM BLACK DRAGON

Now what? You've read the book and you know the power of the information held within. I want you to know that you can help other Public Relations Officers navigate their way through the murky waters of guarding the reputation and managing the publics of their beloved motorcycle clubs on the Biker Set.

If you were helped, educated, or informed by this book there are a couple of simple things you can do to join me in remaking the MC world through knowledge, experience, education, and love:

1. Buy this book for a PRO in your MC. If you believe MC PRO's Bible can deliver good PRO's of your MC then I ask that you spread the word by buying them a copy.

2. Give MC PRO's Bible as a gift or setup a reading group to discuss how MC PRO's Bible applies to the PRO in your MC. You can also write an honest review on social media, your blog, website, or on your favorite bookseller's website. There are countless ways you can help others by spreading this word. PRO's Bible is not just a book worth reading, it's a vision and a plan worth following for every PRO to contribute positively to their MC. It is a vision worth sharing.

3. Enrich other motorcycle clubs by buying this book for your brother and sister MCs on the set with whom you share alliances. Imagine if other PROs could have the benefit of the knowledge you've attained.

Thank you for your support! Send me an email anytime with questions, improvements, or your best PRO tales!